Mr. McIntosh's Family

COVER PHOTOGRAPHS

The photograph on the front cover shows the Eilean Donan castle in the Highlands of Scotland as it appeared in May of 1994. Jacobite soldiers including Brigadier William Mackintosh of Borlum stored gunpowder in the castle during the Rising of 1719. Government forces bombarded the castle, captured the garrison, and used the stored gunpowder to blow up the castle. Early in the twentieth century, the owner of the property rebuilt the castle using the ground plan of the old castle in a reconstruction project that consumed twenty years.

The back cover shows the Castillo de San Marcos in St. Augustine, Florida, as it appeared in July of 1988. Using a local type of limestone called *coquina*; Spanish military officials started building the fort in 1672 and renovated it from 1738 to 1756 during the struggle for the colonial American southern frontier. When John Mackintosh Mor and his son William fought in the Battle of Mosa in 1740, they were part of a British invasion of Florida that failed mainly because the Castillo de San Marcos was essentially unassailable.

Photography by Daniel McDonald Johnson

Mr. McIntosh's Family

The Mackintosh clan
and the McIntosh family
in the Jacobite Risings,
the settlement of Darien, Georgia,
and the struggle for the
Colonial American southern frontier

Daniel McDonald Johnson

Copyright 2022
Independently published by
Daniel McDonald Johnson
Post Office Box 747
Allendale, South Carolina 29810

ISBN: 978-0-578-39969-0

ABOUT THE AUTHOR

Daniel McDonald Johnson has served as the head librarian at the University of South Carolina Salkehatchie since 2009. Previously, he edited the community newspaper in Sylvania, Georgia, and spent more than twenty years as a reporter, photographer, and editor for newspapers in Allendale, Barnwell, Charleston, Ridgeland, and Walterboro, South Carolina.

Johnson holds a bachelor's degree in English and a master's degree in library science, both from the University of South Carolina.

He has written several books concerning Georgia families on the Colonial American frontier and in the American Revolution:

"And at Darien, a most unhappy Accident befell Mr. McIntosh's Family."

Colonial Records of Georgia 4: 165

ACKNOWLEDGEMENTS

When I visited my grandparents Daniel and Lorena "Nina" McDonald in McIntosh County, Georgia, their neighbor Bessie Lewis inspired me to learn about the Scots Highlanders who settled the area. I fondly remember conversations with her and I continue to enjoy the books she wrote.

As I began doing serious research into the exploits of the McIntosh family, Brigadier William Mackintosh of Borlum's descendant Mattie Gladstone of the Ridge in McIntosh County provided me with source material and guided me to historic locations.

More recently, John Mackintosh Mor's descendant Billy McIntosh of Savannah graciously shared fascinating McIntosh family stories with me.

I am grateful to the staffs of the Georgia Historical Society, the Allendale County Library, the Colleton County Memorial Library, the Screven County Library, the University of South Carolina Library System, and the Interlibrary Loan Department of the Thomas Cooper Library at the University of South Carolina.

I appreciate the love, encouragement and support of my wife, my brothers and my sister, and cherish the memory of my parents and grandparents.

Daniel McDonald Johnson

CONTENTS

The Jacobite Risings of 1715 and 1719 ------- 3

John Mackintosh Mor and his uncle Brigadier William Mackintosh participate in the Jacobite Rising of 1715, are taken prisoner at the Battle of Preston, escape from prison and flee to France.

The Brigadier participates in the Jacobite Rising of 1719 and, after the Battle of Glenshiel, remains in the Highlands as a fugitive from the British government.

The settlement of Georgia ------- 33

John Mackintosh Mor, accompanied by his wife and their six children, leads a contingent of Highlanders who establish the town of Darien, Georgia. Aeneas Mackintosh serves in a ranger troop assigned to protect the Highlanders in the new settlements and goes on a trek through Indian country.

The struggle for the southern frontier ------- 57

John Mackintosh Mor and his eldest son William participate in the Battle of Mosa, where John Mor is taken prisoner. William serves in the regiment at Frederica. John Mor's second son Lachlan is placed in an orphanage, and John Mor's wife seeks refuge with a kinsman. Lachlan joins William at Frederica shortly before the Battle of Bloody Marsh. John Mor rejoins his family after three years as a prisoner of war.

(Continued on next page)

The Jacobite Rising of 1745 ------- 109

Aeneas Mackintosh succeeds to the title of 22nd Chief of Clan Mackintosh and marries Anne Farquharson. In the Jacobite Rising of 1745, Aeneas serves in the government army while Anne rallies the clan for the rebels.

The Last Laird of Borlum ------- 151

Edward Mackintosh 7th of Borlum becomes known as the last laird of Borlum. In 1773, Edward disappears after being accused of an armed attack on a cattle drover; his brother Alexander is found guilty of the attack and is executed. The heir of Borlum may be found in the descendants of John Mackintosh Mor.

Transitions ------- 159

The military colonization of Georgia comes to a close and the Highlander soldiers become Georgia planters.

Lachlan McIntosh and his brothers take an active role in the independence movement in Georgia.

Directory ------- 187

Brief biographical sketches can be used in place of an index. The reader can learn which events a particular person was involved in, and then read the relevant chapters.

Notes ------- 193

Bibliography ------- 203

INTRODUCTION

I have adapted *Mr. McIntosh's Family* from my bigger book *Blood on the Marsh*. The bigger book chronicles the epic adventures of General Lachlan McIntosh, Roderick McIntosh, Colonel Anne Mackintosh, Colonel John McIntosh, John Mackintosh Mor, Captain Aeneas Mackintosh and Brigadier William Mackintosh from the Jacobite Risings through the American Revolution. It also tells the stories of Flora MacDonald, Sergeant McDonald of Marion's Brigade, my immigrant ancestor Alexander McDonald of the regiment at Frederica and his son Alexander McDonald, who fought for independence in the American Revolution.

This book focuses on legends involving Clan Mackintosh in Scotland and the family of John Mackintosh Mor, also known as John McIntosh Mohr, in Georgia during the period from 1715 to 1775.

Like the bigger book, this one contains both history and legend. Legends are neither fiction nor nonfiction; they are based on historical events and feature historical people, but they intertwine mythology, folklore, and creative storytelling with historical facts.

Daniel McDonald Johnson
Allendale, South Carolina
July 4, 2014

Mr. McIntosh's Family

The Jacobite Risings of 1715 and 1719

John Mackintosh Mor and his uncle Brigadier William Mackintosh participate in the Jacobite Rising of 1715, are taken prisoner at the Battle of Preston, escape from prison and flee to France.

The Brigadier participates in the Jacobite Rising of 1719 and, after the Battle of Glenshiel, remains in the Highlands as a fugitive from the British government.

The first time John Mackintosh went to war he was not older than 17. He went out in the Jacobite Rising of 1715 with not only his uncle Brigadier William Mackintosh but also his more distant relative Lachlan the 20th Chief of Clan Mackintosh and most of the men and older boys of the clan. To help distinguish young John Mackintosh from the many other clansmen with the same name, his acquaintances added "mor," the Gaelic word for big, after his name.[1]

John Mackintosh Mor's uncle William Mackintosh had served in the French military service and had made friends with a descendant of the Stewart kings of England, Scotland and Ireland. Calling himself James III of England and James VIII of Scotland, and using the French spelling "Stuart" for the dynastic family name, he claimed to be the rightful successor to his father, James II of England and James VII of Scotland. His supporters were called Jacobites, from the Latin word for James.

The last Stewart king had been replaced by a half-sister, Mary, and her husband, William of Orange. Mary's sister Anne succeeded them. When Queen Anne died without an heir, there was a chance that the would-be James III could claim the throne if he converted to the Protestant church but he remained faithful to the Catholic church. Parliament arranged for a German-speaking Hanoverian to be crowned George I; his only qualifications to be King of England were being a great-grandson of James I and, more important, being a Protestant.

When James made a move to reclaim the British crown for the Stuart line of succession, William Mackintosh returned to his homeland in the Scottish Highlands and recruited warriors for the cause. He persuaded Lachlan the 20th Chief of Clan Mackintosh to join the cause and bring out the clan's fighting men – and boys like John Mackintosh Mor, who was either 15 or 17 years old at the time, according to conflicting sources. [2]

The Mackintosh battalion consisted of thirteen companies of fifty men each. Officers were:

Colonel: Lachlan, 20th Chief of Clan Mackintosh.

Lieutenant Colonel: John Ferguson [i.e. Farquharson].

Major: John Mackintosh, third son of Borlum, brother to the Brigadier.

Captains: Laughlin Mackintosh of Knocknagael, second son of the Brigadier, father of John Mackintosh Mor; Duncomb Mackintosh, son of Borlum, brother to the Brigadier; Laughlan Mackintosh, Junior, eldest legitimate son of the Brigadier; Farquhar Macgillivray of Dunmaglass; Angus Macbean of Kinchyle; Robert Shaw, younger of Tordarroch; William Mackintosh; Angus Mackintosh of Killachie; Francis Farquharson of Whithouse; Laughlan Maclean.

Lieutenants: Two persons named John Mackintosh; Benjamin Mackintosh, a natural son of the Brigadier; William Macgillivray, brother to Dunmaglass, and called afterwards 'Captain Baan";

John Farquharson of Kirktown; Farquhar Macgillivray of Dalcrombie; John Macbean; Angus Shaw, second son of Alexander Shaw of Tordarroch; James Mackintosh; William Maquinn [Macquen]; Duncan Mackintosh; John Abercromby (lieutenant and aide de camp); [first name unknown] Skeen; David Stuart; William Mackintosh.

Aide: John Mackintosh.

Adjutant: Daniel Grant.

Paymaster: David Macqueen.

Quartermaster: William Shaw. [3]

The Rising of 1715

The Jacobite rising got underway on September 6, 1715, when the Earl of Mar raised a blue and gold flag at Braemar in the Highlands and proclaimed James VIII to be the rightful and natural king by the grace of God. [4] The Chief of Clan Mackintosh promptly proclaimed King James at Inverness—the largest town in the Highlands, located in Clan Mackintosh territory—and seized all the public money and arms kept in Inverness.

The Mackintoshes then tried to seize the arms and ammunition at Culloden House, home of Duncan Forbes. "Mrs. Forbes, in the absence of her husband, put her house in a state of defence," writes the official Mackintosh historian, "and sent to Munro of Foulis for help. Munro was coming to her assistance when he was stopped by Seaforth, who was on the Jacobite side. However, Seaforth persuaded Mackintosh not to waste precious time storming a single house against a woman, but to march his eight hundred men south to join the Earl of Mar at Perth." [5]

A Jacobite force of twelve thousand men assembled at Perth. Lachlan the Chief of Clan Mackintosh commanded the Mackintosh battalion while William the younger of Borlum gained the rank of brigadier and took command of a brigade.

"It speaks well for the generosity of the Chief that he was willing to serve under his own clansman," writes Margaret Mackintosh of Mackintosh, herself the lady of a clan chief. [6]

Crossing the Forth

Another clan historian tells what happened next:

[The Earl of Mar] conceived the plan of sending a force under Brigadier MacKintosh into England to encourage the Jacobites there. The Brigadier did not approve of the plan, but finding Mar determined upon it, he went into it with his usual wholeheartedness. The force selected for the expedition consisted of six regiments – Lord Strathmore's, Lord Mar's, Logie Drummond's, Lord Charles Murray's, Lord Nairn's and Mackintosh of Mackintosh's. The Brigadier forthwith pressed into his service all the boats along the Northern shore of the Forth, and chose the nights of the 11th and 12th of October for the crossing. As Argyle was in force at Stirling, several men-of-war were cruising in the vicinity, and from eighteen to twenty miles of water to cross in open boats, the undertaking was a perilous one. Nevertheless he succeeded in getting 1500 men, including MacKintosh's regiment, across, a feat even in the present day considered remarkable. Having collected his men, who got scattered in crossing, at Haddington, he daringly resolved to march upon Edinburgh. [7]

A nineteenth-century Scottish historian provides some other details of the expedition:

[Mackintosh] was sent to Burntisland with two thousand men to secure boats with which to cross the army, and while here, on the 9th October, he addressed the following curious and ingenuous letter to Captain Pool of H.M.S. Pearl, then employed in guarding the Firth and its shipping from the designs of the Highlanders:

"Sir, - You lying so near a part of the King's army of which I have the honour to command as Brigadier-General, thinks it incumbent upon me to require, command, and summons you in His Majesty King James the Eighth's name, to come in and return your duty, allegiance, and obedience to him, and does promise you that your early appearance will meet with all suitable encouragement from me, and will entitle you in all time coming to receive from His Majesty such favours as so great a service deserves. If ye incline to hearken to this proposal you'll be pleased to send some officer ashore that I may fully commune with him, and I promise him protection and safety to come and return, and if ye desire I shall send an officer to you upon the like protection granted. The complying with this measure will be just, safe, honourable, and advantageous. The enclosed is the Earl of Mar and others of the nobility and gentry their manifesto calculate for the kingdom of Scotland, and since it has pleased God to bring His Majesty safely into his own kingdoms, ye may expect that encouragement will be given to the Royal Navy of England."

The reply of Pool to the letter of the "Arch rebel," as he calls him, was a threat to lay the place in ashes, but Highland wit proved more than a match for loyal Pool, for ere the English captain awoke next morning Mackintosh had crossed over with his force, and it was firmly established at North Berwick, Aberlady, and other places along the coast. Ere long they held possession of Haddington for King James. The Lord Justice Clerk writing on 13th October, to Secretary Stanhope of these things, says: -

"Lord Nairn and two or three other lords are come over, but it is Mackintosh of Borlum that is the principal man that commands at Haddington. Some of the rebels were at the President of the Session's gate before his family was well awake, and his lordship narrowly escaped; two of his sons were taken, but they have let them go again upon their parole of honour, and Borlum, as Brigadier of the Pretender's forces, gives them a pass, which pass I have seen... This landing is the boldest, and perhaps the most desperate, attempt you ever heard of." [8]

Margaret Mackintosh of Mackintosh picks up the story of the expedition:

Borlum, with fifteen hundred men, including the Mackintosh regiment, succeeded in crossing from Pittenweem and Crail in open boats. The Brigadier promptly marched on Edinburgh, where he hoped to be assisted by the Jacobites within the city. The city magistrates, however, upon hearing of Borlum's approach, had promptly lodged all the leading Jacobites in prison.
Borlum was too experienced a soldier to waste his little army by attempting to carry a big city by assault without any assistance from within, so he seized Leith instead and fortified himself in one of the forts built there by Cromwell. There he

was attacked the following day by Argyll who, failing in his assaults, was compelled to withdraw. Borlum, in obedience to orders received from Mar, thereupon marched his force south to join Lord Kenmore and the English Jacobites under Mr Foster. He found them at Kelso, the Highlanders marching into town playing their pipes. They seem to have inspired the natives with profound terror, and quite a hundred years later the name of Borlum was used as a bogey to frighten children. It must have been merely their wild appearance that produced this effect, for Borlum maintained good discipline.

Lord Kenmure took over supreme command of the army, and Borlum retained command of the Highland division. He advised Kenmure to attack the English under General Carpenter, who was known to be training recruits in cavalry. Kenmure rejected the advice and was to rue his decision…

Borlum was also anxious to join the western clans under General Gordon and so to secure Scotland, rather than to penetrate England, where so far there had been no sign of a rising. His advice was again flouted, as Mr Foster and Lord Widdrington assured Kenmure that all Lancashire, being a nest of Catholics, would rise if the Scots marched in. Kenmure decided to advance into England and march into Lancashire. When the Scots then refused to cross the Border, in loyalty to his General, Borlum personally persuaded about a thousand Highlanders to follow, but five hundred others turned back and went home, though Borlum stood in the Esk swearing at them and calling them "reskels of humanity."[9]

Crossing the Esk

Another clan historian gives a slightly different account of the border crossing:

> When they reached the Border some of the men refused to go into England, and an eye-witness describes the Brigadier standing in the middle of the Esk endeavoring with all his authority and eloquence to prevent them from deserting. We can image the beetle-brow darken, and the grey eyes flash, as he thunders at them "Why the ----- not go into England where there are men, meat and money? Those who are deserting me are but the rascality of my men." [10]

The Battle of Preston: November 12-14, 1715

A Clan Mackintosh historian describes events leading up to the Battle of Preston:

> After crossing the Border, the command devolved upon Foster, the English General, who proved himself wholly incapable, and of no military ability whatsoever. When they reached Penrith on the 2nd November they found a force of rustics estimated at 15,000 assembled to oppose them. Those men, however, were not sufficiently trained to resist the little army of 4000 men from the North and they were soon put to flight. After many councils and cross marches, with which the Brigadier was much disgusted, Forster and his force on the 10th November entered Preston. Here they were joined by 1,200 allies, mainly badly-armed recruits. Forster was elated at this accession to his force, but the Brigadier looked upon it with different eyes. "Look you here, Forster," he exclaimed, "are these

the fellows you intend to fight Wills with? Good faith, Sir, and ye had 10,000 of them I would fight them all with 1000 of his dragoons." At that very time too several parties of Hanoverian troops under Generals Wills and Carpenter were hastening with all speed to Preston. On the night of Friday, 11th November, Forster received intelligence of the approach of Wills, but instead of making preparations to resist the enemy, he retired to bed, leaving the other leaders to arrange for the defence of the town. Notwithstanding this gross neglect of duty he did not hesitate next morning to change the dispositions that had been made, with the result that neither the bridge nor the fords leading to the town were defended, and the enemy was allowed to cross the Ribble unmolested. Across the principal streets, however, barricades planned by the Brigadier were erected. The main barriers were four in number – one a little below the church, commanded by the Brigadier; another at the end of a lane leading into open country, under Lord Charles Murray; a third called the Wind-Mill, under MacKintosh of MacKintosh; and a fourth in the street leading towards Liverpool, commanded by Major Miller. The three first barriers were attacked with great fury, but without success. The attack on the Brigadier's barrier was repulsed with considerable loss to the assailants, and that on Lord Murray's and MacKintosh's were equally unsuccessful. In the back part of the town 300 of Wills' men who tried toward nightfall to enter the "Back Weem," were repulsed with the loss of 140 men killed. The fight continued throughout the night, although the local Jacobites took advantage of the cover of darkness to escape. The original little army was thus left to its fate. [11]

Military historian William Seymour describes the Battle of Preston in his comprehensive book *Battles in Britain*:

> On the night of 9 November the Jacobite horse entered Preston. Two troops of Colonel Stanhope's dragoons, who were in the town, withdrew without offering any resistance.
>
> On 10 November the foot also arrived in Preston, and Forster, who had been assured through his local intelligence system that he could expect ample warning of any enemy approach, intended resting his army for a day or two before proceeding to Manchester. It came as a considerable surprise to him, therefore, to learn on the 12th that General Wills, who commanded the royalist troops in Cheshire, was at hand with five cavalry and three infantry regiments. Moreover, General Carpenter, displaying an offensive spirit that went far to compensate for the inferior material at his disposal, was said to be closing in from the north-east. This information seems to have proved too much for Forster, who issued a series of orders and counter-orders then retired to his lodgings. When, a little later, Colonel Oxburgh and Lords Kenmure and Widdrington reported for orders they found their 'general' in bed.
>
> Preston was a quite unprotected small market town, but a resolute commander could have put up a strong defence. The key point to be held was the bridge over the Ribble and John Farquharson of Invercauld had been sent there by Forster with a small force of picked men. Farquharson had plenty of courage and he and his men would have given a good account of themselves, but at the first hint of danger they were withdrawn to the town. Wills was so amazed at finding the bridge unguarded that he immediately suspected an ambush in the

narrow lane with its high hedges that led from the bridge up the hill to the town. He therefore proceeded with caution, which enabled the Jacobites to perfect their dispositions. These were fairly skilfully laid out, and reflect some other hand than Forster's.

Barricades were set up blocking the main entrances to the town and proper use was made of the houses and narrow lanes as points of defence. The Jacobites possessed six cannon, and if these could have been properly manned the royalists, who were without artillery, would have been more severely mauled than was the case: but without trained gunners what little advantage they offered was chiefly psychological. Brigadier Mackintosh of Borlum commanded the barricade set up to the east of the church in the main street, and was supported by the Earl of Derwentwater's troops, who were in position in the churchyard. Another member of Clan Mackintosh commanded what was known as the windmill barrier, which was situated on the Lancaster road, while the one on the Liverpool road was under a Major Mills. Lord Charles Murray blocked a lane leading into fields across which General Carpenter's troops were expected. By midday on 12 November Preston was in a state of adequate defence.

General Wills, having discovered that the approach lanes to the town were clear and that the Jacobites had decided to make a stand, launched a two-point attack. Brigadier Honywood, commanding his own dragoons, and Preston's foot under Lord Forrester, attacked Borlum's post, while Brigadiers Dormer and Munden led a mixed force of infantry and dismounted cavalry against the Lancaster barricade. Little headway was made against this barrier and the attack does not seem to have been a very spirited affair. But on the Wigan side of town the battle was fiercely contested and the Jacobites, firing from the protection of houses, inflicted considerable casualties on Wills' men.

The strength of Borlum's position was that between the double barricade set up to the east of the church there stood two of the largest houses in the town. These belonged to Sir Henry Haughton and Mr Hare; both houses had been occupied by Highlanders. A frontal attack down the road had no chance of success so long as the attackers were subject to enfilade fire from these houses; but when Lord Forrester infiltrated his regiment through the gardens between the church and the two houses the position was dangerous but by no means critical – that is, until the troops in the larger house (Haughton's) were withdrawn. It is not clear from contemporary accounts of the battle why Mackintosh did this, but it was a fatal error. Before nightfall Preston's regiment was in possession of both these houses, although in getting them they suffered the only heavy casualties of the whole battle.

A third attack had also been launched against Lord Charles Murray's barricade, but this had been held after heavy fighting in the course of which Murray had to ask for reinforcements from Derwentwater. As night drew on and the whip-lash sound of close-range bullets became less persistent the Jacobites could be well content with the day's work, for all the barriers were still intact, although the one by the church had become dangerously vulnerable. However, all was not well among the rebel soldiery: royalist prisoners taken in the fighting soon dispelled all hopes that any of their colleagues would desert. Some Jacobites with cool heads, and cold feet, made their way out of the town while there was still time – for the next day General Carpenter arrived and immediately sealed off all exits.

Carpenter claimed the credit for the victory, but at the time he commended General Wills for the fighting on the 12th, and the only serious flaw that he could find in his dispositions was that the bridge and ford across the Ribble had been left unguarded. Once these exits had been closed the rebels were bottled up, but there was little doubt that they could have fought their way out. However, much to the disgust of the Highlanders, caitiff counsels in the end prevailed.[12]

Margaret Mackintosh of Mackintosh reports the Highlanders' violent resistance to surrender:

The Chief of Mackintosh commanded one defence force, Borlum another... Things were not going so badly with the Jacobites at first, until Wills was reinforced by General Carpenter, whom Kenmure had neglected to destroy. This was too much for Foster, who gave up all hope and, without the knowledge of the Scots, sent a secret envoy to Wills to ask for terms. Wills ordered their surrender as rebels and demanded two leaders as hostages – one Scottish and one English. Accordingly the Chief of Mackintosh and the Earl of Derwentwater were placed in Wills' hands.

The Highlanders, on finding the surrender arranged 'were terribly enraged, and declared they would die fighting.' They killed a good many who dared to talk to them of surrender. However, their fury was unavailing, and on Wills threatening with his superior force to kill every man of them the inevitable surrender took place. [13]

British military historian William Seymour resumes his account of the Battle of Preston and its aftermath.

On 14 November the English marched in and disarmed Forster's men. The number of prisoners taken was about 1,500, of which seventy-five were English noblemen or gentlemen and 143 Scottish. Most of the rank and file taken were Scotsmen and they were treated with considerable savagery. The important prisoners were taken to London and some were sentenced to death... The Jacobite casualties were only eighteen killed and twenty-five wounded, as opposed to about 200 royalists killed or wounded, most of whom were from Preston's regiment.

The Battle of Preston terminated the Jacobite insurrection in England; but at almost exactly the same time as Forster and his officers were negotiating the surrender in Lancashire an even more disastrous blow to James's cause was struck on a lonely moor near Stirling. [14]

Battles decide the Rising of 1715

The Jacobite Rising of 1715 resulted in two major battles fought at the same time, one at Sheriffmuir in Scotland and the other at Preston in England.

On November 13 at Sheriffmuir near Stirling, 3,100 men led by the Duke of Argyll attacked the Jacobite army of 7,100 men under the Earl of Mar. Argyll's outnumbered men fought Mar's army to a draw, halting Mar's advance toward England and influencing many of his soldiers to desert the Jacobite cause.

Mackintoshes taken prisoner at Preston

Margaret Mackintosh of Mackintosh tells the fate of her clansmen after the collapse of the Jacobite Rising of 1715:

General Wills took possession of Preston with fifteen hundred prisoners – of the rank and file were sixty bearing Clan Chattan names, including thirteen Mackintoshes and sixteen Macgillivrays.

The Chief and Borlum and others of note were sent to London, but many of inferior rank were executed, and others transported to America for slavery, while some were imprisoned in various English towns.

The officers sent as prisoners to London were escorted from Highgate in a mock triumphal procession followed by a jeering mob. Mackintosh is described as 'a brave and handsome gentleman,' and Borlum as 'remarkable for the grim ferocity of his scarred face.' For five months they lay in prison until in April 1716 their trial was to be held. On the night before this trial Borlum and fifteen others overpowered the sentinels and made their escape from prison; seven were recaptured, but the others, including Borlum, got safely away. Foster escaped in a separate venture. The Government issued a description of the Brigadier as 'a Tall Rawboned Man about sixty years old, Fair-Complexioned, Beetle-Browed, speaks Broad Scotch.' They offered one thousand pounds reward for Borlum's capture, but he evaded pursuit and was assisted by his brother-in-law,

Thomas Reade, in Oxfordshire, to conceal himself until he was able to find a ship to carry him to France.

The London mob, with whom Borlum was decidedly popular, was highly pleased with his escape. They celebrated his heroism in ballads not flattering to their countrymen. The following ballad is quoted from Hogg's *Jacobite Relics of Scotland*:

Mackintosh was a soldier brave
And did most gallantly behave
When into Northumberland he came
With gallant men of his own name…

Old Mackintosh he shook his head,
When he saw his Highland lads lie dead;
And he wept not for the loss of those,
But for the success of their proud foes.
Then Mackintosh unto Wills he came,
Saying, 'I have been a soldier in my time,
'And ere a Scot of mine shall yield,
'We'll all lie dead upon the field.'

'Then go your ways,' he made reply;
'Either surrender, or you shall die.
'Go back to your own men in the town:
'What can you do when left alone?'
Mackintosh is a gallant soldier,
With his musket over his shoulder.
'Every true man point his rapier:
'But, damn you, Foster, you are a traitor!'

… Brave Derwentwater he is dead;
From his fair body they took the head;
But Mackintosh and his friends are fled,
And they'll set the hat on another head.
And whether they are gone beyond the Sea,
Or if they bide in this country,
Though our King would give ten thousand pound,
Old Mackintosh will scorn to be found.

…The Chief of Mackintosh was released from prison in 1716, at the intercession of his wife and Lord Lovat and other friends, who pleaded that Lachlan had been 'trepanned into the rebellion by the craft of the Brigadier'!

After his release in 1716, the chief devoted himself to improving his estates and to settling disputes. [15]

At least eleven Jacobite prisoners named Mackintosh were transported from Liverpool to South Carolina in the spring of 1716. [16]

Borlum is dead; long live Borlum

In the Highlands of Scotland, William Mackintosh 3rd of Borlum – father of Brigadier William Mackintosh and grandfather of John Mackintosh Mor – died in 1717. The Brigadier, as the elder son, was entitled to the designation 4th of Borlum but not to ownership of the estate. His father, anticipating that the government would seize the property of Jacobite gentry, had arranged in January of 1715 for the estate to pass to the Brigadier's elder son, Lauchlan. When the 3rd of Borlum died, Lauchlan inherited the estate and the designation 5th of Borlum. Lauchlan's uncle Lauchlan

Mackintosh of Knocknagael – father of John Mackintosh Mor – served as the young laird's Curator. [17]

The Borlum branch of Clan Mackintosh had been founded by a son of Lachlan, known as Mor, the 16th Chief of Clan Mackintosh. Lachlan's oldest son had died – but not before fathering a future chief of the clan – and his remaining adult sons did not abide by his wishes. Margaret Mackintosh of Mackintosh gives the details:

> Lachlan had trouble with his sons, who did not uphold their father's reconciliation with Campbell of Cawdor, and more especially after his eldest son's widow married Donald Campbell. Malcolm and William Mackintosh twice raided Cawdor's lands and disputed their sister-in-law and her husband's liferent for Dunachton. Cawdor's sons were brought as prisoners to the Chief of Culloden, who at once released them. He was very much displeased with his sons, whom he refused to see for a year. William was put in prison and the Clan Mackintosh had to pay a considerable fine as a penalty to the Crown. The fiery William established himself at Borlum about four miles outside Inverness on the east bank of the River Ness. He thus founded the colourful and important Borlum branch of the Mackintosh clan. A story is told that the wife of one of the early Mackintoshes of Borlum incited her two sons to murder the Provost of Inverness. Her reason was that this gentleman, on seeing her in the town one day, was so shocked by her 'rude and indelicate demeanour' that he had said, 'Oh, fie, fie, fie Lady Borlum' thus rousing her deadly fury! [18]

The first Laird of Borlum was succeeded by his son Lauchlan who was succeeded by his "eldest lawful son" William as the 3rd of Borlum. William married Marie Baillie of Dunain. Their first son William would become known as the Brigadier. A clan historian provides biographical details:

> William the Brigadier, 4th of Borlum, possessed the estate of Raits, in Badenoch, and married, in 1688, Mary, daughter of Edward Reade, of Ipsden, Oxford, who was, prior to her marriage, a Maid of Honour, to Princess Anne, afterwards Queen Anne, and had issue, Lauchlan 5th of Borlum, Shaw 6th of Borlum, Winwood, Maria Forbes, and Helen. Probably owing to his absence on military service, very little is known of his early life... [19]

About two years before his marriage, the Brigadier became the father of a natural son, Benjamin. [20]

The third son of William the 3rd of Borlum became known as Lachlan Mackintosh of Knocknagael. He married Mary, daughter of John Lockhart of Inverness.

Their first child, born in 1698 or 1700 in Badenoch, was named John and would be known as John Mor. He had a younger brother, Alexander, and a sister, Jane.

Their mother died in 1713 – two years before John Mor marched off to war with his uncle the Brigadier – and was buried in the Grey Friars Inverness. [21]

The Brigadier participates in the Rising of 1719

Brigadier William Mackintosh the younger of Borlum found refuge in France for a few years after the Rising of 1715. Some people say that teenage John Mackintosh Mor "was in France with his uncle, the old Brigadier McIntosh." [22]

Before long, however, both of them were back in their native country. A pamphlet printed in 1718 explaining the reasons for a standing British army reported "that peril was already looming in Scotland, Brigadier MacKintosh's ghost having been seen in the Highlands." [23]

Within a year after his ghost was spotted, the Brigadier appeared in the Highlands in the flesh as part of a renewed attempt to fulfill his friend's desire to rule as James III of England and James VIII of Scotland.

James had formed an alliance with the King of Spain after England had declared war on Spain in 1718. Spanish officials planned an invasion of England with twenty-seven ships and five thousand men while a diversionary force of Spaniards and British Jacobites would go to Scotland to rally the Highland clans to the Jacobite cause.

Storms prevented the Spanish invasion of England, however, leaving the diversionary force to face its fate alone. In the spring of 1719, a force of 307 Spanish soldiers and a few British Jacobites – including Brigadier William Mackintosh of Borlum – sailed to Loch Alsh opposite the Isle of Skye on the west coast of the Scottish Highlands and unloaded their arms, powder and supplies at Eilean Donan Castle. The two Spanish frigates that transported the force returned to Spain.

Leaving a few Spanish soldiers to guard Eilean Donan, Jacobite leader the Earl Marischal established his position nearby.

The government took action to keep Brigadier Mackintosh's clansmen from coming out to support him. The "Shirreff principal of the Shirreffdom of Inverness" summoned a number of clansmen – including Angus Mackintosh of Killachy, Lachlaine Macintosh younger thereof, and William Macintosh of Aberarder – to give security for their peaceful behavior. [24]

The Rising of 1719 had started inauspiciously and would end ingloriously. In *The Jacobites*, Frank McLynn writes:

> On 9 May 1719 events took an ugly turn. A British squadron sailed into Loch Alsh, overwhelmed the forty-five-strong Spanish garrison, blew up Eilean Donan Castle, captured its store of munitions, and burned the stores.
>
> With few provisions, an acute shortage of ammunition and no means of retreat, Marischal had to withdraw inland. No doubt it was his intention to reach Inverness, but the Hanoverian General Wightman advanced down the Great Glen and cornered the Jacobite army at Glenshiel.
>
> Although Seaforth's Mackenzies had risen and a handful of MacGregors under Rob Roy, Marischal's force numbered no more than 1,000. Wightman had no great advantage in numbers but he had a formidable battery of cohorn mortars, which tore holes in the Jacobite ranks. The Highlanders melted away into the hills, but the Spaniards were forced to surrender. All the Jacobite commanders made good their escape. Such was the fiasco of the '19. [25]

The Battle of Glenshiel: June 10, 1719

Twentieth-century military historian William Seymour gives details of the Battle of Glenshiel:

> About six miles south-east of Loch Duich the high hills on each side of the present road almost join; here the road, then nothing more than a cattle drove, winds through a pass not fif-

ty yards wide. It was a place where a handful of resolute men might have held up an army for days. The Jacobites arrived at this pass towards the end of May...

...The Jacobite right, under Lord George Murray, took up a position in the foothills immediately to the south of the drove, with advance patrols some way forward. The 250 Spaniards held the rocky hillside immediately north of the drove, and above them came Lochiel and his 150 clansmen, then forty of Rob Roy's rascals, and further up were men under commanders such as Sir John Mackenzie, Brigadiers Campbell of Ormidale and Glendaruel, and Brigadier Mackintosh of Borlum. Lord Seaforth, with 200 of his best men, was in a commanding position about half a mile up the steep hill.

Against this Jacobite force of 1,600 Highlanders and 250 Spaniards, General Wightman had 850 foot, 120 dragoons and 136 Highlanders. This was no country for cavalry, so the dragoons had been dismounted on entering the glen. They, together with the six coehorn mortars advanced along the line of the drove. On the extreme right Wightman placed his Mackays from Sutherland, then came some 200 Grenadiers under Major Richard Milburn, the 11th and 15th Foot, and a Dutch contingent. This right wing was commanded by Colonel Clayton, whose own regiment, under Lieutenant-Colonel Reading, formed part of the left wing, which advanced south of the drove with the Monros on the extreme left.

The engagement began on the Jacobite right soon after midday, when Lord George Murray's advance picquets contested ground as they gradually fell back onto the main position, but it was not until after 5 p.m. that the battle proper began. Undoubtedly the mortars played an important part in this short fight. They were used in the first instance against Lord George's men, who promptly withdrew from the very exposed hillock to the south of the drove, thus leaving the pass virtually unguarded. They were then turned upon the Spaniards, and firing at extreme range they probably did little harm, but they set the heather on fire, which must have caused confusion in the ever-narrowing funnel of attack. Meanwhile the Mackays, having made light of the steep and rocky ascent, had got round Seaforth's flank, and in the short bout of musketry that followed the Earl got a ball in the arm. Soon the Jacobite left was in retreat, and although the Earl Marischal and Brigadier Campbell of Ormidale held the centre steady for a while it was not long before these men, and then Lord Tullibardine with the Spaniards, were seen to be scampering up the hillside and away through the pass that leads round the north side of the Sgurr na Ciste Duibhe. Before darkness fell on 10 June 1719 the Jacobite army had disintegrated and the Pretender's troops in Scotland had suffered the last of the repeated blows of fortune.

The surprising ease with which the King's army rolled up the rebels is no indication of the Highlanders' inability to hold an almost impregnable position. The fact is that this was just a face-saving affair. The will to win was lacking, for no one would have known what to do with a victory had it been gained. The battle was chiefly notable in that it was probably the only one in which Highlanders fought without charging or engaging in hand-to-hand grapple. The Spaniards, being unable to melt into the countryside, had to surrender, but the battle casualties were quite insignificant. Wightman lost twenty-one killed and perhaps double that number wounded, while there is no reliable record of any Jacobites being killed. However, some there must have been; and no doubt the figure of less than ten mentioned in Field-Marshal Keith's memoir is about right. Lord George Murray was among those wounded, but he soon recovered and almost thirty years later, when another and more romantic Jacobite prince resolved to venture upon the hazards of invasion, he was to play a most important part. [26]

"Captain Downe, of Montague's regiment, was killed," Dr. J.J. Galbraith told the Gaelic Society of Inverness in 1928, "and buried by the river side, where, under the name of the Duitseach he still walks at night. The Spaniards killed are said to have been buried in Clachan Duich under Leac nan Spainteach." [27]

Colonel Jasper Clayton, who commanded the left wing of the government forces, commended the conduct of the Scots Highlanders who served with him. "Lord Strathnaver's and Culcairn's Highlanders behaved perfectly well," he wrote, "but poor Culcairn is shot in the thigh, but not in danger." [28]

Jacobite leader the Marquis of Tullibardine mentioned both "Brigadeer M'Intosh" and "Major McIntosh" in an eyewitness account of the battle:

> My Lord Seaforth met us and told me he had brought to the Crow of Kintaile about five hundred of his own men who, it was thought, would heartily defend their own Country.
>
> On the eighth Rob Roy's son brought a Company of men who, with some volunteers, made up near Eighty.
>
> That night we got accounts the enemy were removed from Gilly whining to the Braes of Glenmoriston, which made us

march early next morning, till that part of the pass at Glenshellbegg, which every body thought the properest place for defence, in which we posted ourselves the best way we could...

Next morning [the government troops] were decamp'd and moving slowly forward. About ten a Clock fifty more men joined us, and at twelve Mckinnin came with fifty more which were the last, for tho' several men that were to be with us (were) on top of the mountains on each side, yet they did not descend to incorporate with the rest. I suppose because they thought the Enemy too near us...

We had drawn up to the right of our main body on the other side of the water upon a little Hill about one hundred and fifty men, including the Companys of my Lord Seaforths, besides above four-score more were allotted for that place who was to come from the top of the Hill, but altho' they sent twice to tell they were coming, yet they only beheld the action at a distance. This party was commanded by Lord George Murray, the Lord of MacDougal, Major McIntosh, and John of Auch, ane old officer of my Lord Seaforths people; at the pass on the other side of the water were first on the right the Spanish Regiment which consisted of about two hundred men, about fifty more of them were left behind with the Magazine, several of them being Sick. The next in the line was Locheill with about one hundred and fifty.

Then Mr Lidcoats and others, being one hundred and fifty, twenty volunteers, next fourtie of Rob Roy's, fiftie of MacKinnins, and then two hundred of my Lord Seaforths men Commanded by Sr John MacKenzie of Coul; on the left of all at a considerable distance on a steep hill was my Lord Seaforth posted with above two hundred of his best men, where my Lord Marshall and Brigadeer M'Intosh commanded with the Spanish Colonel, Brigadeer Campble of Glenderwell and myself commanded in the center, where we imagin'd the main attack would be, it being by far the easiest Ground, besides the only way through the Glen.

However, it happened otherways, the Enemy placed there horse on the low Ground, and a battalion of them on there left, with there Highlanders on the fare side of the water, all the rest of there foot was on a rising ground to there Right.

The first attack they made was on our men with Lord George on the Right, by a small detachment of Red coats and there Highlanders, who fired several times at each other without doeing great damage, upon which they sent a second and third detachment that made most of those with Lord Geo. run to the other side of a steep Burn where he himself and the rest were afterwards obliged to follow, where they continued till all was over, it being uneasy for the enemy to pass the hollow Banks of that Burn.

When they found that party on our Right give way there Right began to move up the Hill from thence, to fall down on our left, but when they saw my Lords Seaforths people, who were behind the steep rock, they were oblig'd to attack them least they should be flank'd in coming upon us, upon which the Laird of Coul (most of whose men began to goe off on the seeing the enemy) mov'd up with his Battalion to sustain the rest of the McKenzies, which oblig'd the Enemy to push the harder that way, on which my Lord Seaforth sent down for a Reinforcement, and immediately after Brigadeer Campble of Ormondell came likewise, telling it was not certain of there main body would not just then fall upon our Centre, which made Rob Roy with the Mcgrigors and MacKinnin the longer of drawing off to there assistance, but seeing them give way he made all the dispatch he could to join them. But before he could get up, so as to be fairly in hands with the Enemy, Lord Seaforths people were mostly gone off, and himself left wounded in the Arm, so that with difficulty he could get out of the place.

Rob Roy's detachment, finding them going off began to retyre. Likewise, that made us still send off fresh supplys from our left, so that Mr Lidcoats men and others seeing every body retire before them, did also the same, and the enemy, finding all give way on that hand, they turn'd there whole force there, which oblig'd us to march up the Camerons, who likewise drew off as others had done; at last the Spaniards were Called and none standing to Sustain them, they likewise were obliged to draw up the hill on our left, where at last all began to run, tho' half had never once an opportunity to fire on the Enemy, who were heartned on seeing some of ours give way, and our people as much discourag'd, so that they could never be again brought to any thing. But all went off over the mountains, and next morning we had hardly any body togeither except some of the Spaniards.

...The Spaniards themselves declared they could neither live without bread nor make any hard marches through the Country, therefore I was oblig'd to give them leave to Capitulate the best way they could, and every body else went off to shift for themselves... [29]

When the other Jacobite leaders fled Britain, Brigadier Mackintosh chose to abide in his homeland. He "kept out of the way" of government authorities and remained in Scotland for years. [30]

Brigadier Mackintosh imprisoned

Brigadier William Mackintosh of Borlum "lingered for some time in his native land" after the Rising of 1719. "There he was at length captured and imprisoned in Edinburgh Castle."[31] A clan historian writes:

> In 1729, about the time of his incarceration, he published an "Essay on Ways and Means for Inclosing, Fallowing, and Planting in Scotland," and by the manner in which it is written one can judge that not only had he a perfect command of English (Gaelic would have been the language of his childhood), but that he was quite at ease with Latin and Greek from his many references to the classics. That he was a born soldier and a brave gentleman no one will deny. [32]

Chief of Borlum goes to America: 1721

Because the Borlum estate was deep in debt, John Mackintosh Mor's cousin Lauchlan Mackintosh, 5th of Borlum, "decided to try his fortune in New England, and left Scotland in 1721 for Darien, where his grand-uncle, Col. Henry, had settled many years before," reports a clan historian.

Lauchlan married Col. Henry's daughter, Elizabeth, shortly after arriving in America. Their first daughter, Elizabeth, was born in 1722. [33]

The Jacobite Risings of 1715 and 1719

Borlum is dead; long live Borlum

In the summer of 1723, Lauchlan, 5th of Borlum, planned a visit to Scotland while his infant daughter and pregnant wife remained at their home in New England. Lauchlan drowned at sea; his wife gave birth to their daughter Mary two months later. In Scotland, Lauchlan's brother Shaw succeeded as 6th of Borlum. [34]

Mackintosh is dead; long live Mackintosh

Lachlan the 20th Chief of Clan Mackintosh died in 1731 at Moy, the clan seat. The official clan historian describes the succession:

> The funeral was delayed for two months owing to the absence of his successor, and the body lay in state at Dalcross. As with previous funerals of Mackintosh chiefs, the expenses were enormous, and burdened the estate for years. Several thousand persons attended the burial at Petty.
>
> William, the twenty-first Chief, succeeded in 1731. He was a second cousin of the late Chief, and a great-grandson of Sir Lachlan, the seventeenth Chief.
>
> William had been in the Army, but he now set himself to relieving the estate of its burdens, and he cleared off some two thousand pounds in debts. For this reason, the Reverend Lachlan Shaw says, 'he did not effect the clannish grandeur, the numerous attendants and servants, common among Highland chieftains. He abridged the number of servants and cut off much of the superfluous expenses of his family.' Shaw also says, 'His life was a pattern of virtue and goodness.'
>
> In those days it was the custom to fight duels, and William fought his share. At this time an officer named Graeme had possession of Dundee's sword, which Lachlan had given up to

him after the battle of Preston. William challenged Graeme either to give up the sword, or fight a duel, but fortunately Captain Graeme agreed peacefully to return the famous sword, which is still preserved at Moy Hall. [35]

John Mackintosh Mor faces family duties

John Mackintosh Mor—a nephew of the Brigadier and a first cousin of Shaw the 6th of Borlum—married Marjory, daughter of John Fraser of Garthmore, on March 4, 1725, at Dores.

When their first child was born on January 27, 1726, at Borlum, they named him William—a family name shared by John Mor's grandfather the 3rd of Borlum and uncle the Brigadier. [36]

Their second son was born on March 5, 1727, in Achugcha, near Raits in Badenoch. Given a family name – shared by his grandfather Lachlan Mackintosh of Knocknagael and another ancestor Lachlan, known as Mor, the 16th Chief of Clan Mackintosh – the child was destined to become known as Continental General Lachlan McIntosh.

John Mackintosh Mor pursued his career as a gentleman farmer by moving from place to place but never leaving Mackintosh clan territory, as indicated by the birthplaces of his children. The third son—named John like his father—was born in 1728 at Ballochroan near Kingussie in Badenoch.[37] The fourth son Phineas was born while the family lived at Ardo. About two years later the twins Lewis and Janet were born on November 4, 1734.

John Mackintosh Mor's father Lachlan Mackintosh died January 29, 1735, and was buried at Grey Friars Inverness. [38]

The settlement of Georgia

John Mackintosh Mor, accompanied by his wife and their six children, leads a contingent of Highlanders who establish the town of Darien, Georgia. Aeneas Mackintosh serves in a ranger troop assigned to protect the new settlements established by his relatives.

Fort established on Altamaha River

The Highlanders who were banished to South Carolina after the Jacobite Rising of 1715 arrived in a war-torn colony on the colonial American southern frontier. In what was called the Yemassee War, strong forces of southern Indians sought to exterminate South Carolina. The Indians found allies among French colonists to the west and Spanish colonists to the south.

As a defensive measure, Colonel John Barnwell of South Carolina persuaded the British government to post soldiers in the debatable land between the British colony of South Carolina and the Spanish colony of Florida. In 1722 the Independent Company of Foot established Fort King George at the mouth of the Altamaha River. "The ill-conceived fortification was designed to prevent the French from controlling the Altamaha River region and to guard the southern frontier from attacks by Spaniards and Yemassee Indians," writes Larry Ivers in *British Drums on the Southern Frontier*. "However, the French were not then capable of such expansion efforts, and the fort did not prevent the movement of Yemassee war parties from their sanctuary in Spanish Florida to South Carolina." [1]

Mackintosh clansman serves in South Carolina

A high-ranking member of Clan Mackintosh serving in the British military was posted on the colonial American southern frontier in 1732. Known by both the Gaelic name Angus and the classical name Aeneas, he was a brother of William the 21st Chief of Clan Mackintosh. He was stationed at Fort Prince George, also known as Palachacola Fort, on the Savannah River upstream of the tidewater. Military historian Larry Ivers explains the significance of Palachacola:

> Palachacola had long been a strategic point on South Carolina's southwestern frontier. The name was derived from Palachacola Town, a settlement of friendly Apalachicola Indians, which had served as a sentry-town, guarding the principal crossing site on the lower Savannah River. However, when the Yemassee War began in 1715 those Indians joined the conspiracy against South Carolina and were soon forced to vacate Palachacola Town and flee to their ancient home in present southwestern Georgia. Without a guard on the lower Savannah crossing site, war parties could cross the river and penetrate the settlements at will. The Company of Southern Rangers (1716-1718) built a fort across the river from the abandoned town and patrolled along the east bank of the Savannah River during the first six months of 1718 in an attempt to secure that portion of the frontier...
>
> For a while Palachacola lay unguarded, but in early 1723 the settlers living north of Beaufort began clamoring for government rangers to protect their plantations from the raids of Yemassee war parties operating from Spanish Florida. In February the South Carolina government ordered a captain, a

lieutenant, a sergeant, and nineteen horsemen to be recruited to build and garrison a "small Pallisade Fort" at Palachacola. They were to range east above Beaufort and north to Fort Moore [further upstream on the Savannah River], keeping the Indians west of the Savannah River...

The Palachacola Garrison was instructed to patrol the one hundred miles of frontier between Port Royal and Fort Moore once every two weeks, but it appears very unlikely that they actually covered the terrain that often, if ever. During the period of brutal Indian raids, 1726-28, the garrison's patrols did not discourage all the Yemassee war parties from crossing the Savannah River and penetrating the settlements...

During a Creek Indian scare in August 1732... the Palachacola Garrison went on full alert. Colonel Alexander Glover, the Creek Indian agent, rode to Fort Prince George and assumed command of that section of the frontier. Even though Captain Evans, the commander of the fort, had been too sick to perform duty for some time, he had still been retained in command; however, when war with the Creeks seemed likely Evans was discharged and Lieutenant Parmenter was promoted to captain. Aeneas Mackintosh, a Scottish gentleman and heir to the chieftainship of Clan Mackintosh in Scotland, was commissioned lieutenant. At the end of the first week in September the fear of a major Indian war dissolved when the government discovered that the Creeks had no intention of going to war. [2]

The British colonization of Georgia

In response to French and Spanish threats to British colonies in North America, as well as Indian raids from Florida into South

Carolina, the British Board of Trade authorized fortified settlements along the southern frontier. The plan eventually resulted in the founding of Georgia. Larry Ivers explains:

> Two townships were supposed to have been located near the Altamaha River in old Guale, the virtually uninhabited Atlantic coastal area that was hotly claimed by both England and Spain, but their establishment was delayed until the task was undertaken by the new colony of Georgia during the period 1733-36.
>
> The colonization of Georgia was timely for the British defense of the southern frontier...
>
> The Georgia project was the fusing of two requirements into one solution The first requirement was philanthropic. James Oglethorpe, Dr. Thomas Bray, Sir John Percival, and many other Englishmen considered colonization one of the best methods of solving the problems of Britain's debtors, unemployed, and poor. This coincided perfectly with the second requirement, military colonization of the Altamaha-Savannah Rivers region as ordered by the Board of Trade. Slavery was prohibited in Georgia; villages of white protestant yeomen, planting crops and training as soldiers, were to act as a buffer against the Spaniards in Florida and the French in Louisiana. [3]

Aeneas Mackintosh protects new settlement

The rangers on the colonial American southern frontier – including Aeneas Mackintosh, a brother of the Chief of Clan Mackintosh – provided protection for the first settlers of Georgia. In *British Drums on the Southern Frontier*, Larry Ivers describes the role of the rangers:

About the latter part of January 1733 a messenger from Charles Town rode his horse into Saltcatchers Fort at the head of Combahee River on the South Carolina frontier and delivered a message to Captain James McPherson, the commander. Inside were marching orders from the governor. "You... are hereby order'd immediately with fifteen men to repair to the new Settlement of Georgia, there to Obey orders and directions as you Shall receive from Mr. Oglethorpe, in order to Cover and protect that Settlement from any insults; of this fail not."

At that moment 113 people, newly arrived from England, were temporarily camped in Fort Frederick at Port Royal, South Carolina, awaiting transportation to the southern bank of the Savannah River where they planned to establish a new British colony called Georgia. South Carolinians correctly viewed the new settlement as a godsend; it would absorb the bloody raids of the Florida Spaniards and their Yemassee Indian allies which had previously been directed against South Carolina. A grateful South Carolina General Assembly had provided the new colonists with boat transportation, breeding cattle and hogs, provisions, and military protection by the provincial scout boat and Captain McPherson's Company of Southern Rangers.

... [Rangers] selected riding and pack horses and strapped provisions and ammunition to pack saddles. Captain McPherson chose six of the company's twenty privates to remain in garrison at Saltcatchers Fort. Within a few days they were reinforced by the temporary assignment of a lieutenant and four rangers from Fort Prince George on the Savannah River...

The company probably began its movement to Georgia at dawn one day during the first week of February 1733. The governor had made preparations for the rangers to ride to the Savannah River, cross on riverboats called piraguas, ride down the western bank, and then rendezvous with the Georgians. The path was a new one, a ride of over forty miles which followed the ridges and crossed a number of creek swamps, perhaps a two-day journey for the rangers and their pack horses. They probably spent a night at Purrysburg, a new frontier "township" of Swiss immigrants on the east bank of the Savannah River. The next morning they pulled and shoved their horses onto the piraguas which had been assembled to transport them down river to the Georgia settlement...

The Georgia colonists had already landed at Yamacraw Bluff on Thursday, 1 February ...and were laying out a settlement called Savannah. James Oglethorpe, the Georgia trustee who acted as the colony's leader, was proceeding under the advice of Colonel William Bull, a prominent South Carolina frontiersman. When the rangers rode into the Georgians' camp they found them hard at work hacking a town out of the wilderness. A third of the men were clearing trees from the town site, another third were working on a blockhouse, and the remainder were clearing land for the planting season just a month away. Cold rain fell in torrents that February, making working conditions miserable...

Oglethorpe stationed the company up river about five miles northwest of Savannah at a place called the Horse Quarter from where they patrolled the area close around Savannah during the remainder of the winter and spring of 1733. [4]

In early February 1733 one of the Southern Rangers from Saltcatchers rode into Fort Prince George [at Palachacola on the Savannah River] with the governor's message concerning the measures to be taken to protect the Georgia settlers. According to the governor's order, Captain Parmenter sent Lieutenant Mackintosh and four men to strengthen the remaining garrison at Saltcatchers Fort, leaving both garrisons with ten men each.

...By March 1734 the South Carolina government realized that the organization of frontier defense would have to be permanently altered because of the settlement of Georgia. The rangers at Saltcatchers were needed in Georgia and were ordered to join McPherson there. Lieutenant Mackintosh and his men demolished Saltcatchers Fort, probably setting fire to the huts and palisade to prevent its being used by hostile Indians.

South Carolina disbanded Captain Parmenter's Palachacola Garrison, but Oglethorpe placed four of his men in Fort Prince George to maintain the buildings and cannons... The South Carolina settlers on the frontier near Port Royal were outraged by the removal of all the soldiers from their portion of the frontier, and to pacify them the government in Charles Town ordered Mackintosh and his ten rangers to station themselves at Fort Prince George [on the South Carolina side of the Savannah River at Palachacola] instead of Fort Argyle [a new ranger fort on the Ogeechee River in Georgia].

Under the new establishment Mackintosh was promoted to captain and his men became known as the Palachacola Rangers. They patrolled the eastern bank of the Savannah River as part of Captain McPherson's Company of Southern Rangers until April 1735... [5]

Mackintosh assists Mackay

As the commander of Fort Prince George at Palachacola, Captain Aeneas Mackintosh was called upon to assist Patrick Mackay as Mackay began a journey into Creek Indian territory. Ivers describes the mission:

> The Lower Creek were often troublesome to the British, but in the spring of 1734 they were addressing a loyalty of sorts to Georgia because James Oglethorpe had met with some of their headmen during the previous year and had established a treaty of friendship with the help of Tomochichi, the Yamacraw mico (chief), and a large amount of presents. The trustees' Indian policy was initially wise and fruitful. They lavished presents on the Indians, redressed the Indians' grievances wherever possible, and acquired land through treaty rather than appropriation.
>
> Oglethorpe was the perfect man to carry out the trustees' policy. He ate the Indians' food, slept in their houses, sincerely recognized their value as Georgia's allies, and seldom voiced impatience with their alien-appearing customs...
>
> ...Oglethorpe wrote a captain's commission for Patrick Mackay, his choice to command the company destined for duty in the Creek nations...
>
> On 15 August 1734, after a summer of frustrating dealings with a hostile Charles Town, Captain Mackay set out overland for Georgia with the herd of horses... On the third day the packhorsemen became so ill that Mackay was forced to camp near the Ashepoo River for two days while they partially recovered. ...two of the packhorsemen had relapses and were

left alongside the road to recover. Mackay and his two remaining men had considerable difficulty in driving the herd, which probably consisted of about fifty horses of the tough breed raised by the Cherokee. During the week it took to travel from the head of the Ashepoo River to Palachacola on the Savannah River, several horses escaped and drifted into the swamps.

Finally, on 26 August, Captain Mackay rode into Fort Prince George at Palachacola with his horses. Captain Aeneas Mackintosh, the garrison commander, lent Mackay two of his rangers to help corral the herd and tend it until the packhorsemen were well enough to rejoin Mackay. The piragua arrived soon afterward and its cargo of presents and equipment was secured in the fort. [6]

After Mackay left Palachacola to join the company of men allocated for his mission, he discovered that all of them suffered from a fever. Mackay himself became delirious with fever and lay in bed for two weeks in Savannah. In October he went to Beaufort, suffered a relapse and "lay near death for twenty days." His expedition into Creek territory finally got underway in November. [7]

Recruiter entices clansmen to Georgia

When Oglethorpe determined to establish a fortified settlement on the Altamaha River in the debatable land claimed by both England and Spain, he sent recruiters to Clan Mackintosh country. Oglethorpe had other links to the Mackintosh clan in addition to his dealings with Captain Aeneas Mackintosh in America. Oglethorpe's mother, Eleanor Wall Oglethorpe, was a Jacobite sympathizer. Oglethorpe's sisters married into the French Catholic aristocracy and had connections with the Stuart court. Oglethorpe himself may have met Brigadier William Mackintosh of Borlum and his nephew John Mackintosh Mor when the three of them were in France. [8]

McIntosh County local historian Bessie Lewis says that Oglethorpe chose Highlanders to defend the southern frontier because of their reputation as fierce fighters:

> In January, 1734, James Edward Oglethorpe, his Savannah settlement well on its feet, made a journey down the coast. He carefully inspected the mouth of the Altamaha and its environs, saw the ruins of old Fort King George and the need for a fortified town at this place. It was then that he decided Scottish Highland warriors – men whose willingness to "face cold steel" was legend – were the settlers he wanted there.
>
> Under his orders, Captain Hugh Mackay and Captain George Dunbar spent the next few months in the Highlands near Inverness, recruiting men and families for this settlement.[9]

Georgia historian Edward Cashin describes the recruitment process in *Lachlan McGillivray, Indian Trader*:

> The summer of 1735 was an opportune time for Captain George Dunbar and Hugh Mackay to come to Inverness to recruit men for Georgia in America. A succession of poor crops had reduced gentlemen and tenants alike to poverty. The town council of Inverness thought so well of the idea of sending a hundred or so hungry men to Georgia that it made Georgia's founder, James Oglethorpe, an honorary burgess of the town. The authorities were even more pleased that the emigrants

were Jacobites. Dunbar was wise to the ways of his native shire. He obtained the support of William Mackintosh, chief of Clan Chattan [a confederation of clans led by the Mackintoshes], for the venture. The chief was called Mackintosh of Mackintosh, and he lived at Moy Hall... He borrowed money on his lands to assist the gentlemen who should go to Georgia. Most of them were chosen for their leadership qualities. Outstanding among them was John Mohr Mackintosh, who had gone off to fight in 1715 with his uncle Brigadier [William] Mackintosh of Borlum... Dunbar's tactic, as Oglethorpe explained it to his fellow Trustees of Georgia, was "to bring the enterprise into vogue with the chief gentlemen" so as to secure their tenants. He was fully aware that these gentlemen "were unused to labour," and therefore each had to bring a man capable of working. John Mackintosh of Holme, aged twenty-four, with the chief's money and his own, paid for himself and sixteen-year-old Lachlan McGillivray. Lachlan's aunt Magdalen was married to William Mackintosh of Holme, brother to John. Seventeen gentlemen paid their own passage on Dunbar's ship the *Prince of Wales*, and the Georgia Trustees paid for 146 others.

Among the emigrants was a confusion of Mackintoshes. Besides John Mohr Mackintosh of Borlum and John Mackintosh of Holme, there were John Mackintosh of Kingussie, John Mackintosh of Dornes, John Mackintosh Bain, and John Mackintosh Lynvilge. The McGillivrays were represented by Lachlan, his cousin Farquhar, aged thirty, and Archibald, aged fifteen.

Why would the Mackintosh of Moy Hall pay to speed the departure of his clansmen? For one thing, his brother Aeneas

Mackintosh was already in Georgia in the service of James Oglethorpe. In 1735 this Aeneas was stationed at a fort on the Carolina side of the Savannah River to protect the new German settlement at Ebenezer, forty-five miles above Savannah. The agricultural depression undoubtedly was a factor in the migration of so many from the same district. It has been suggested that Mackintosh would never have been able to enclose his lands for sheep raising if the likes of John Mohr Mackintosh still occupied the estates.

In going to Georgia, Lachlan McGillivray was not running away from home... He was going with his clan to join others already in Georgia and Carolina. He must have felt a touch of nostalgia as the blue-green hills faded from view, but he must also have felt the quickening flush of adventure.[10]

Like Cashin, the official historian of Clan Mackintosh stresses that the exodus to Georgia was a clan affair rather than a series of individual choices:

During William's chiefship an important emigration took place. General James Oglethorpe, the English philanthropist, had obtained a royal grant of lands in what is now the Savannah area of Georgia in order to colonise it with distressed persons such as debtors or sufferers from religious persecution, both from England and continental Europe. After founding the colony in 1733 Oglethorpe was soon in difficulty with the Spanish in neighbouring Florida, who claimed the land. To stiffen his colonists he decided to recruit Highlanders with strong military potential. In 1735 he... carefully selected men of good character willing to go to America. These men were led by John Mor Mackintosh, a nephew of Brigadier Mackintosh of Borlum and thus related to the Mackintosh Chief, described as a gentleman farmer. Also in the party were Roderick and John Mackintosh, grandsons of the Brigadier, and many other Mackintoshes. They took their whole families with them, and the better off also took their servants. Their willingness to go at all may be partly accounted for by the depressed state of the Highlands and it seems likely that William encouraged his clansmen to go. On 18th October 1735 the good ship *Prince of Wales* commanded by Captain George Dunbar sailed from Inverness with 200 Highlanders, 50 women, and some children. On arrival they called their settlement New Inverness, but later changed it to Darien in memory of the ill fated Darien expedition of the end of the seventeenth century.[11]

Going to Georgia with the grandsons of Brigadier Mackintosh – John and his younger brother Roderick, probably about 20 years old – were their younger sister Winnewood and their father Benjamin, about 50 years old. Lady Mackintosh may be too polite to mention Benjamin because he was a natural son of the Brigadier born two years before the Brigadier was married.[12] Benjamin, being a son of the Brigadier, was a first cousin of John Mackintosh Mor.

John Mackintosh Mor was about 37 years old when the emigrants set sail and his wife Marjory was about 34. Of their nine children, six remained alive in 1735: William, age 9; Lachlan, 8; John, 7; Phineas, 3; and 11-month-old twins Lewis and Janet.[13]

Highlanders settle in Georgia

The emigrants who set out to sea from Inverness in mid-October of 1735 made landfall at Savannah in early January of 1736. Local historian Bessie Lewis imagines the arrival of Scots Highlanders in the lowcountry of coastal Georgia as "Scene I" in *They Called Their Town Darien*:

> A chill wind blew over the marshes of the Altamaha delta as the small boats – manned by sturdy Scottish Highlanders and a few of Tomochichi's Indians – came up the river to Barnwell Bluff that 19th day of January, 1736. As they rounded the last bend before the high bluff they saw just ahead the ruins of Old Fort King George and all that was left of the landing used by the Independent Company nine years before.
>
> Pulling close to the point, they tied up the boats and disembarked. Here the land was low, and the kilted Highlanders with their Indian friends walked to the high bluff adjacent, where they could look out over the vast Altamaha delta. In Savannah they had been told by would-be troublemakers that at this place Spaniards would shoot them upon the ground from their houses in the fort. And the Highlanders had replied, "Why, then, we will beat them out of their fort and shall have houses ready built to live in."
>
> But there were no houses in sight, only that vast expanse of marsh interlaced with the waters of the Altamaha – they would have to build their own houses.
>
> This group was the vanguard of the "177 heads" of Scottish Highlanders... The women and children, with the older men, were left in Savannah while the able bodied men and the indentured servants went on down the Inland Waterway to the

site selected by James Edward Oglethorpe for their settlement. There they were to build huts and shelters for the comfort and protection of their families and a chapel in which their minister, the Rev. John McLeod, would hold divine services on Sundays and teach the children on weekdays.

First they mounted their "great guns" on the ruins of Fort King George in case Spaniards or enemy Indians should approach. Then they set to work to build accommodations for families.

The work went on – soon the huts and shelters were ready and the rest of the Highland embarkation came to join the settlement at Barnwell's Bluff. Already they had named their town Darien.

On Sunday, the 22nd of February, 1736, James Edward Oglethorpe made his first visit to the Highlanders who had been recruited under his special orders for this settlement. They met him in full military regalia, and in their honor he wore the kilt. In a letter to the Trustees for the Establishment of the Colony of Georgia, reporting on that visit, he wrote, "I arrived at the Scotch settlement, which they desire may be called Darien. They were all under arms and made a most manly appearance, with their Plads, broad Swords, Targets [a type of shield used by Highlanders was called a targe or a target] and Firearms."

There on the bluff the Highland Company paraded before him, in the first formal military review in the colony of Georgia.

Thus was founded the town the Highlanders called Darien...

Oglethorpe spent but one day and night in Darien on his first visit, but it was long enough to convince him that he had been wise in his selection of Highlanders for this strategic point on the Altamaha. He found them to be what he had requested and expected, "the Freemen of Gentlemen's families... Industrious, laborious and Brave; speaking the Highland language."

They were the McIntoshes, led by John McIntosh Mohr; the Mackays, headed by Hugh Mackay; the McDonalds, Morrisons, Sutherlands, and others. They were soldiers, schooled in war and ready and willing to fight. Hugh Mackay held a commission in the British army, as did James Mackay; John McIntosh Mohr had been in battle at the age of fifteen.

As Oglethorpe was pleased with the settlers of Darien, so they were with him, giving him on that first visit a warm affection and fierce loyalty which was to endure throughout his stay in Georgia... He asked nothing of his men but what he would himself endure.

This was proven on his first night in Darien. Hugh Mackay offered him a bed in his own tent, with sheets, but Mr. Oglethorpe refused, and wrapping himself in his plaid lay down by the guard fire outside. Mackay and the other officers joined him, though the night was cold.

Before Oglethorpe left Darien on the occasion of his first visit, Mr. McPherson, with a detachment of the rangers, arrived overland from Savannah, pleasing the Highland settlers with the knowledge there was communication for horsemen between the two towns.[14]

Another account says that Oglethorpe slept beneath "a great tree;" consequently a huge live oak tree in Darien became known as the Oglethorpe Oak.[15]

"Oglethorpe arrived at Darien, so well coached by Dunbar that he wore a plaid. Kilts had not yet been introduced to the Highlands," points out Georgia historian Edward Cashin, "and the men wore a fourteen-foot-long swath of cloth gathered at the waist and falling freely to the knees, the loose ends pinned at the left shoulder to leave the right arm free to brandish a sword."[16] Cashin continues:

> Captain Hugh Mackay had the nominal military command, but the real authority figure in Darien was John Mohr Mackintosh. Oglethorpe soon discovered that he could deal with the Gaelic-speaking indentured servants only through their leaders. Because they spoke no English, they could not be dispersed among the other settlements. John Mackintosh set them to work clearing fields and planting corn before he let them build houses...
>
> Although the Highlanders managed to raise enough corn that first year to supply themselves, farming was not their long suit. They were not good at it in Scotland, and they were less proficient in America, where they had more excuses for leaving off such disagreeable labor. They much preferred cutting down trees and sawing wood for their own houses and for their sister settlement, Frederica, on St. Simon Island. They must have wondered at the number and size of the tall sea pines and the girth and spread of the giant oaks. There were more trees in Darien than in all of Invernesshire in Scotland.[17]

Indians and Highlanders form friendships

In *Lachlan McGillivray, Indian Trader*, Edward Cashin explores the bonds that developed between Scots Highlanders and American Indians on the colonial American southern frontier:

> A party of curious Creek Indians went to see the Highlanders even before Oglethorpe arrived in Darien. The Indians and the Scots got along famously from the start. They discovered that they shared the same values. The clan system was not unlike the tribal divisions. Status was the product of kinship and prowess. The manly arts were esteemed in both cultures, both had their war songs, their traditional dances, their reciters of the great deeds of the past. The Gaels and the native Americans were born storytellers, given to flights of imagery and metaphor. The world of spirits was real to both cultures. The mutual respect led to friendly competition in an American version of the Highland games as Scots vied with Creeks in feats of swiftness, strength, and dexterity.
>
> [John Mackintosh Mor's son] William Mackintosh... recalled in later life that a quick friendship developed between the visitors and the men of Darien. We can picture the Scottish lads engrossed in their efforts to communicate with the young warriors, first in sign language and then in sound recognition. We can only guess at the wonder they felt as they were introduced to a culture as rich and proud as their own. Both William [McIntosh] and Lachlan [McGillivray] learned the language of the Creeks. William later became a planter on the Georgia coast, but Lachlan was intrigued by the glimpses into the world of the Creeks. He had relatives [in South Carolina] already engaged in the Indian trade. He would join them as

soon as he had satisfied his obligations to his patron, John Mackintosh of Holme.

The Highlanders learned more about their situation from the Indians than they did from the busy Oglethorpe. They were aware of the threat from the Spanish in St. Augustine and from their Indian allies. Some of the Darien men accompanied Oglethorpe on his reconnaissance through the debatable land below the Altamaha River. Highlanders were posted on Amelia Island at the entrance to the St. Johns River. They called their fort St. Andrews [after the patron saint of Scotland] and the island Highland and bid defiance to the dons. They knew that Oglethorpe was preparing Frederica as his garrison town for the inevitable war.[18]

John Mackintosh Mor's son Lachlan was "of athletic form and great activity," an early Georgia historian writes, and "when a lad at New Inverness, there was not an Indian in all the tribes that could compete with him in the race." This information came from the historian's grandfather William McIntosh, the older brother of Lachlan McIntosh.[19]

Highlanders raise black cattle

Raising and raiding cattle provided money and excitement for Highlanders in Scotland. Following their ancient custom, the Highlanders in Darien raised black cattle to provide beef for the soldiers at Fort Frederica on St. Simon's Island. Captain James McPherson – who was born in South Carolina but still bore a Highland name – drove the first herd of cattle to Darien from South Carolina.[20]

In addition to raising cattle, McPherson served with Aeneas Mackintosh as a ranger on the southern frontier. While stationed at Saltcatchers Fort in southern South Carolina, McPherson established a five-hundred-acre cattle ranch near the fort.

When Georgia was founded, McPherson and Mackintosh were sent to protect the new settlements; McPherson's wife managed the cattle herd and the corn crops while McPherson was away on assignment.[21]

Nieces of Laird of Borlum settle in Georgia

John Mackintosh Mor's cousin Shaw 6th of Borlum sailed from Scotland to New England in 1736 to visit the two daughters of his late brother Lauchlan, who had immigrated to New England and started a family before his death at sea.

Shaw tried to persuade his nieces to come to Scotland. His nieces, however, found husbands in America and settled in Georgia.[22]

The birth of Ann McIntosh

A child was born to John Mackintosh Mor and his wife Marjory a little more than a year after they arrived in Georgia. Their daughter Mary Ann, called Ann, was born on April 18, 1737.[23]

Their family now contained five sons – William, Lachlan, John, Phineas and Lewis – and two daughters – Janet, the twin sister of Lewis, and newborn Ann.

More Highlanders settle in Georgia

General Oglethorpe authorized ongoing efforts in the Highlands of Scotland to recruit fighting men for fortifications and watchposts along the Georgia coast and to obtain servants for the colonists. About forty Highlanders, representing twenty-six different clan names and perhaps including a piper or two, arrived at Darien in November of 1737 aboard the *Two Brothers*.[24]

Another ship, the *Mary Ann*, sailed to Georgia in 1737 carrying five recruits for the Independent Company of Foot. One of the recruits, Alexander McDonald, brought along his wife Mary.[25]

Alligator kills son of John Mackintosh Mor

Marjorie and John Mackintosh Mor's twin children died shortly after the family settled on the colonial American southern frontier. A note in the family Bible simply said Janet died young at Darien. Her twin's death was reported in 1738 by an official in Savannah: "And at Darien, a most unhappy Accident befell Mr. McIntosh's Family, whose two Sons (young Lads) being swimming in the River, an Alligator snapped one, and carried him quite off."[26] The official did not name the two children who were swimming, but the alligator's victim had to have been 3-year-old Lewis because the other sons were still alive after 1738. Based on the statement that both boys were "young lads," 6-year-old Phineas may have experienced the horror of watching Lewis being dragged away in an alligator's jaws. If William, age 12, Lachlan, 11, or John, 10, witnessed Lewis's gruesome demise, the older brother certainly would have felt that he had failed to protect his little brother.

Highlanders oppose slavery: 1739

Oglethorpe and his fellow trustees forbade slavery in Georgia for humanitarian and military reasons. Georgians who envied the wealthy slave-owning planters of South Carolina agitated for a change in the trustees' policy. Local historian Bessie Lewis describes John Mackintosh Mor's role in supporting the trustees:

...As a leader of his people, an arbitrator of disputes and one whose opinions were respected, he must take a strong part in this controversy. If nothing else, his loyalty to Oglethorpe demanded he do so. On a night in January [1739], he sent his eldest son, William, a lad of twelve, out to the houses of the town, calling a meeting at his home. Eighteen men responded, and their names are affixed to a unique document... It is a petition against the importation of Negro slaves. The men of Darien gave their reasons for this protest – all were sound and practical. There were five paragraphs in the petition – and the fifth reads like a prophecy: "It's shocking to human Nature, that any Race of Mankind, and their Posterity, should be sentenced to perpetual Slavery; nor in Justice can we think otherwise of it, that they are thrown amongst us to be our Scourge one Day or another for our Sins; and as Freedom to them must be as dear as to us, what a Scene of Horror must it bring about! And the longer it is unexecuted, the bloody Scene must be the greater."

...We who look back through the pages of history and read the tragedy which came to Darien in the 1860's, cannot but wonder if the Highland Scots who signed that petition possessed the second sight that is legend among the Gaels.[27]

The "sound and practical" arguments against slavery in Georgia mentioned in Bessie Lewis' narrative are:

I. The Nearness of the Spaniard, who have proclaimed Freedom to all Slaves who run away from their Masters, makes it impossible for us to keep them without more Labour in guarding them, that what we would be at to do their Work.

II. We are laborious, and know that a White Man may be by the Year more usefully employed than a Negro.

III. We are not rich, and becoming Debtors for Slaves, in case of their running away or dying, would inevitably ruin the poor Master, and he become a greater Slave to the Negro Merchant, than the Slave he bought could be to him.

IV. It would oblige us to keep a Guard-duty at least as severe as when we expected a daily Invasion; and if that was the Case, how miserable it would be to us, and our Wives and Families, to have an Enemy without, and more dangerous ones in our Bosom!

The fifth paragraph continues after the section quoted by Bessie Lewis: "We therefore, for our own sakes, our Wives and Children, and our Posterity, beg your Consideration, and intreat, that instead of introducing Slaves, you'll put us in the way to get us some more of our Countrymen, who with their Labour in time of Peace, and our Vigilance, if we are invaded, with the Help of those, will render it a difficult thing to hurt us, or that Part of the Province we possess. We will ever pray for your Excellency, and are, with all Submission..."

The leader of the Highlanders signed his name as John Mackintosh Moore. Other signers are: John Mackintosh Lynvilge; Ranald M'Donald; Daniel Clark, First; Alexander Clarke, Son to the above; Donald Clark, Third, his Mark; HM Hugh Morrison's Mark; John McDonald; John Macklean; John Mackintosh, Son to L.; John McIntosh Bain; James McKay; Jos. Burges, his mark; Donald Clark, Second; Archibald AMB McBain, his mark; Alexander Munro; William Munro; John Cuthbert.[28]

The birth of George McIntosh

Marjory, the wife of John Mackintosh Mor, gave birth to a boy on May 24, 1739. He was their first son born after they arrived in Georgia and they named him George. Their family now contained five sons – William, Lachlan, John, Phineas and George – and their 1-year-old daughter Ann.

The struggle for the southern frontier

After trekking through Indian country, Aeneas Mackintosh returns to Scotland. John Mackintosh Mor and his eldest son William participate in the Battle of Mosa and John Mor is taken prisoner. William serves in the regiment at Frederica. John Mor's second son Lachlan is placed in an orphanage, and John Mor's wife seeks refuge with a kinsman at Palachacola. Lachlan joins William at Frederica shortly before the Battle of Bloody Marsh, where Highlanders play a major role in a victory against Spanish forces. John Mor rejoins his family after three years as a prisoner of war.

Aeneas Mackintosh treks across Creek Country

Ranger captain Aeneas Mackintosh accompanied Georgia's founder General James Oglethorpe on a three-month, five-hundred-mile journey to and from Creek Indian towns on the Chattahoochee River. Military historian Larry Ivers describes the expedition:

> On 8 July [Oglethorpe] left Frederica accompanied by a few officers of the Forty-second Regiment and some Scottish gentlemen including Lieutenant George Dunbar, Adjutant Hugh Mackay, Jr., and Aeneas Mackintosh. After traveling by boat to Ebenezer they transferred to horseback and rode north to the Uchee town where Lieutenant John Cuthbert and his party of six rangers were waiting to act as the expedition's escort. The rangers had just finished blazing a trail from Augusta to the Uchee town along the west bank of the Savannah River. The

expedition now consisted of Oglethorpe, twelve officers and gentlemen, Cuthbert and his rangers, about five servants, and an unknown number of Indians who served as hunters and guides. Oglethorpe also hired an additional ranger, probably Thomas Hunt, to accompany him as a bodyguard-servant...

They left the Uchee town on 24 July... On 8 August the expedition arrived at Coweta and received a very cordial welcome from Chigelley, the principal mico of the Lower Creek. Chigelley was a warrior to be reckoned with. Twenty-four years earlier he had led a war party of several hundred Creek and Apalachee to within twelve miles of Charles Town, South Carolina, leaving ashes and death behind him. During the next two and a half weeks Oglethorpe was treated as a very important guest of the towns of Coweta and Kashita where he held several councils during which he passed out presents and exchanged speeches with the headmen of both Creek nations. Even the men of his expedition served as diplomats. On one occasion while they were watching the Indians dance, traders' rum or the primitive beat of the drums induced some of them to compliment the Indians by joining in the rhythmic stomping. The visit was extremely timely and may have been partially responsible for the Creek maintenance of neutrality during the subsequent war with Spain and France. The results were probably disappointing to Oglethorpe, however, for he had hoped that the Creek would provide him with large war parties for use in raiding Florida.

On 25 August Oglethorpe and his expedition began their return to the coast, initially setting out on the Lower Trading Path toward the Savannah River, arriving at Augusta eighteen days later. Even though Oglethorpe became sick with a fever he inspected Fort Augusta, ...visited with Captain Daniel Pepper of South Carolina's nearby Fort Moore, and talked with several Cherokee headmen who came down from their nations to receive presents.

On 13 September, a rumor arrived at Augusta that war had been declared against Spain. Four days later, after Oglethorpe and his expedition had started down river toward Savannah, they met a trading boat whose crew was carrying the terrifying news that some Negro slaves in South Carolina had revolted a few days before. South Carolinians, outnumbered by their slaves and living in fear of a revolt for more than a quarter of a century, had taken elaborate but ineffective measures over the years to keep the slaves unarmed, uneducated, and unorganized. The slave insurrection took place west of Charles Town on Stono River where Angola-born slaves who lived in that neighborhood had banded together, armed themselves, and killed twenty-three people. The local militia quickly cornered them, killed about forty, despite their brave stand, and scattered the remainder in the swamps.

...When Oglethorpe arrived at Fort Prince George, or Palachacola Fort, across the river from the Uchee town he found thirty South Carolina militiamen from Purrysburg in garrison. The obvious objective for the rebellious slaves was Saint Augustine – the Spanish governor had promised freedom for all slaves who escaped to Florida – and the principal route to Saint Augustine crossed the Savannah River at Palachacola. In fact, some of Captain James McPherson's slaves had recently escaped on stolen horses from his Saltcatchers plantation, crossed the river at Palachacola, and ridden nearly unhindered through Georgia to Florida. Oglethorpe ordered Captain Aeneas Mackintosh, the former commander of the fort and a member of the expedition, to recruit and command a new ten-man garrison of rangers for Fort Prince George.[1]

A ranger who accompanied Oglethorpe on the journey to the Lower Creek towns of Coweta and Kashita recorded the day-to-day progress of the expedition:

His Excellency Genl. Oglethorpe making a Tour into the Indian Nations to Establish Peace between them and the English ordered me to attend him it being about four Hundred Miles through the Woods...

July the 24th. The General set out with about twenty Five Persons in Company and some Indians all well Armed, it being very Necessary so to be, for not long before a Party of the Choctau Indians came down to the General who gave them Presents and they staid amongst the English as Friends, but did not prove so, for in their Return home, they met two English Men who traded among the Indians, one of these they killed and shot three of the others Fingers off, however he made his Escape to a Town of the lower Creeks, Who upon hearing his Relation of what the Choctau's had done, immediately charged them, killed a great many and took the rest Prisoners. The General had also at this time two of the Choctau Indians with him who had put themselves under his Protection for fear of the People of the Creek Nation who would have killed them for the Barbarity of their Countrymen to the two English Traders. But now I return to our Journey, which we Continued being Supplied with Venison by the Indian Hunters, and also Wild Honey of which they took Plenty.

July 27th. We arrived at Great Ogeechee River which we Swam our Horses over and The Packhorse Man got his Things over in a Leather Canoe which they carry for that Purpose and at every River where they are to use it, they stretch it with Stakes made on Purpose.

July the 28th. The Things being all got over the River we set forward, The Indians killing plenty of Deer and Turkeys for our Refreshment, also several Buffaloes, of which there is great Plenty and they are very good Eating. Though they are a very heavy Beast they will out Run a Horse and Quite Tire him.

July 31st. We Travelled over many Hills from which we had a very Pleasant Prospect of the Valleys which abounded with fine green Trees and abundance of Grapes and other Fruits, but which were not Ripe. From the Top of one of these Hills we perceived a great Smoke at a Distance from us, which we Imagined to be at the Camp of a Party of Spanish Horse which were sent out on Purpose to hinder us if possible from going to make this Treaty of Peace with the Indians and which has since been of so great Service to us, the Friendly Indians annoying the Spaniards very much. We encamped at Occomy River where we found a Horse belonging to one of the Spaniards; We crossed the River and killed two Buffaloes of which there are abundance, We Seeing Several Herds of sixty or upwards in a Herd. We Camped at Ocmulgas River where there are three Mounts raised by the Indians over three of their Great Kings who were killed in the Wars.

August the 6th. We came to Dollus Rivulet where we Encamped; In the Night came to us Capt. Wiggin, Mr. Gudell, and two of the Chief Indians, before they came to us they hooped which our Indians Answered, then they came to our Camp and saluted the General in a very friendly Manner which he Returned.

August the 7th. We set forward and on our way we found several strings of Cakes and Bags of Flower etca. which the Indians had hung up in Trees for our Refreshmt.

August the 8th. We Encamped about two Miles from the Indian Town, The Indians sent Boys and Girls out of their Town with Fowls, Venison, Pompions, Potatoes, Water Melons, and Sundry other things. About ten of the Clock we set forward for the Indian Town and were met by the Indian King And some of their Chiefs, the King had English Colours in his hand. We Saluted them and they Returned our Salute, and then shaking Hands with the General and Company the King very gracefully taking him by the Arm led him towards the Town, and when we Came there they Brought us to Logs which they had placed for that purpose Covered with Bear Skins and desired us to sit down which when we had done The head Warriours of the Indians brought us black Drink in Conkshells which they presented to us and as we were drinking they kept Hooping and Hallowing as a Token of gladness in seeing us. This Drink is made of a Leaf called by the English Casena (and much Resembles the Leaf of Bohea Tea) It is very Plenty in this Country.

Afterwards we went to the Kings House or rather Hut where we Dined, at night we went to the Square to see the Indians dance, They dance round a large Fire by the beating of a Small Drum and Six Men singing; their Dress is very wild and frightfull their Faces painted with several sorts of Colours their Hair cut short (except three Locks one of which hangs over their Foreheads like a horses fore Top) they paint the Short Hair and stick it full of Feathers, they have Balls and rattles about their Waist and Several things in their Hands, Their Dancing is of divers Gestures and Turnings of their Bodies in a great many frightfull Postures.

The Women are mostly naked to the Waist wearing only one short Peticoat which reaches from their Waist a little below their Knees, they are very nice in Smoothing and putting up their hair, it is So very long when untied that it reaches to the Calves of their Legs.

Their Houses or Hutts are built with Stakes and plaistered with Clay Mixed with Moss which makes them very warm and Tite.

They dress their Meat in Large pans made of Earth and not much unlike our Beehives in England. They do not make use of Mills To grind their Corn in, but in lieu thereof use a Mortar made out of the Stock of a Tree which they cut and burn hollow and then Pound their Corn therein, and when it is pounded sufficiently they seperate the husks from the Meal by sifting it thro' a Sieve made of Reeds or Canes.

The Chief Business of the Women is Planting Corn and other things and minding the Business of the House, The Men Hunt and Kill Deer, Turkeys, Geese, Buffaloes, Tygers, Bears, Panthers, Wolves and several other Beasts whose Skins they sell to the Traders for Powder Ball and what other Necessaries they want.

August the 12th. We set out from this Town which belonged to the Couettaus to go to a Town of the Causettaus; As we drew near the Town the King came with English Colours in his Hand attended by his Chief Men, We saluted them and they returned the Salute; The King and his Chief Men conducted the General to their Square where he dined and after Dinner the General went to Captain Wiggins House where he lay that Night.

August the 17th. The Indians went into the Square to Dance and some of the English Danced with them which pleased them very well.

August the 21st. His Excellency General Oglethorpe went to the Square to give the Indians the Presents he had Caused to be brought for them, and to Establish that Peace with them which has since been so Beneficial to the English; He also settled the Trade between the Indians and the Traders.[2]

The Highlanders on the expedition witnessed orders from General Oglethorpe protecting Creek lands from encroachment by colonists. Aeneas Mackintosh signed his name to the document as "Eneas Mackintosh, Esq., Brother to the Laird of Mackintosh." Other Highlanders signing beneath the statement "Made in the square at Coweta Town and in the square at the Cussita Town and translated by a sworn interpreter in the presence of the within mention Indians and under mentioned Britons, and by me" included "Mr. Robert McPherson, brother of Thomas McPherson of Darhade; Mr. John Mackintosh, son of John Mackintosh of Holmes; Mr. James Mackqueer, son of James Mackqueer of Corsbrough; Mr. Kenneth Bailie, son to John Bailie of Balbrobart; Mr. John Mackintosh; Mr. John Cuthbert of the County of Inverness, North Britain."[3]

Aeneas Mackintosh departs for Scotland

Captain Aeneas Mackintosh learned in February of 1740 that his older brother had died or was dying and Aeneas would inherit the estate at Moy, the title of Chief of Clan Mackintosh, and the leadership of a confederation of clans called Clan Chattan. He went from Palachacola to St. Simons Island to inform Oglethorpe that he was going to Scotland. Oglethorpe gave the commission to succeed him as commander of the fort at Palachacola to Aeneas's brother John Mackintosh. Aeneas returned from Savannah to Palachacola, turned over command to his brother, and then left Georgia for Scotland.[4]

War erupts on the southern frontier

General Oglethorpe returned to Savannah from his trek across Creek territory. On September 27 he received a letter from King George announcing that war was imminent between England and Spain and instructing Oglethorpe to "annoy" the Spanish forces in Florida and to defend the English colonies of South Carolina and Georgia. After taking measures to implement the king's instructions, Oglethorpe moved south to his military headquarters at Frederica on St. Simons Island. Larry Ivers, who developed an understanding of military issues while serving as an infantry officer and living "in a primitive earthen walled fort with Vietnamese provincial soldiers," describes the opening incidents of the war that erupted on the southern frontier of colonial America:

> Before dawn on 13 November 1739 about a dozen Yemassee Indians silently beached their dugout canoes on the west side of Amelia Island. The warriors cautiously advanced through the woods and thickets to the northwestern end of the island

until they were looking across a space of cleared ground at the silhouette of Amelia Fort's stockade and house. The war party concealed itself inside the woods near the path that led from the fort and hoped a man would stray into their ambush.

Garrisoning Amelia Fort were sixteen Highland indentured servants who belonged to the trustees and served as scouts aboard Francis Brooks's scout boat Amelia, a sergeant's guard of twelve men from Oglethorpe's Forty-second Regiment, and about ten women and children. Adjutant Hugh Mackay, Jr., the commander, was temporarily at Frederica. After sunup two Highlanders, John Mackay and Angus Macleod, left their warm beds to gather wood for the breakfast fire. Although neither man was feeling well they had not shirked their duty. Unarmed and unsuspecting, they walked out of the fort's gate and up the sandy path into the pines where the war party was hidden. They probably had little time to react before they were shot down by a volley from the Indians' trade muskets. The war party hacked off the Highlanders' heads and carried them off, scalping them as soon as time permitted. Startled from their slumber by the gunshots, the Highlanders and regulars attempted to pursue the Indians, but they were too late. The Indians escaped in their dugouts and paddled safely toward Saint Augustine with their trophies.

Five days after the raid Oglethorpe surrounded Amelia Island with several small boats while he and a detachment of soldiers searched the woods, thickets, and dunes for skulking Indians. They found none. An officer and a platoon of regulars reinforced the fort and Oglethorpe returned to Frederica to continue preparations for the invasion of Florida.

Two weeks after the first raid on Amelia Fort, Spanish Indians repeated their performance and may have killed two more men... In the style that became typically Oglethorpe, he gathered about two hundred regulars, rangers, militia and Indians under his personal command for a raiding and reconnaissance thrust into Florida.

The rangers who were ordered to accompany the raiding force were members of a new unit, the Troop of Highland Rangers, which had been raised on 19 November 1739. The troop numbered about a dozen men commanded by Adjutant Hugh Mackay, Jr., who thus held commissions in both the Forty-second Regiment and the Georgia provincials. The rangers had been recruited from the Highlanders at Amelia Fort and Darien.

The raiding party embarked in fourteen boats on 1 December 1739. During the ensuing two and a half weeks they inflicted very little material damage on the Spaniards; two lookout huts were burned, several cattle were destroyed, and one man was killed. However, Oglethorpe and his officers did familiarize themselves with the terrain immediately south and east of the Saint Johns River and they gained confidence as a result of the Spaniards' timid reaction... [5]

The British raiding party returned to Frederica on December 18, but two scout boats continued to harass Spanish outposts along the St. Johns River.

General Oglethorpe, meanwhile, planned a full-scale attack on the Spanish stronghold at St. Augustine.

Lachlan McIntosh placed in orphanage

John Mackintosh Mor and his wife Marjory placed their son Lachlan and their daughter Ann in the orphanage at Bethesda near Savannah in February of 1740. Lachlan was on the verge of turning 13, and Ann was no older than 3. Records do not explain why children who weren't orphans were placed in an orphanage. An obvious reason is that John Mackintosh Mor anticipated going off to war at any time. He commanded the militia at Darien, and war had erupted between British and English forces on the colonial American southern frontier. While he was away on military service, his wife would be solely responsible for raising four sons, ranging from 14-year-old William to the infant George. The Mackintoshes may have sent Ann to safety because she was the only girl in the family. Since family tradition holds that Marjory wanted her sons to be well educated, she may have viewed Bethesda as a boarding school for Lachlan.[6]

A report from the Orphan House dated June 4, 1740, gives an idea of Lachlan's daily routine:

> They [the orphans] rise about five o'clock, and each is seen to kneel down by himself for a quarter of an hour, to offer up their private prayers from their own hearts; during which time they are often exhorted what to pray for, particularly that Jesus Christ would convert them, and change their hearts.
>
> At six all the family goes to church, where a psalm is sung and the second lesson expounded by Mr. Whitefield, or in his absence an exposition of it is read out of Henry or Burkitt by the president.
>
> ...Between seven and eight we go to breakfast in the same room with the children, who sometimes sing a hymn before,

sometimes after and sometimes both before and after every meal, as well as say graces.

During breakfast the business of the day is talked of and each appointed his station and perhaps some useful questions are asked the children, or exhortations given them.

From eight to ten the children go to their respective employs, as carding, spinning, picking cotton or wool, sewing, knitting. One serves the apothecary, who lives in the house, others serve in the store or kitchen; others clean the house, fetch water, or cut wood. Some are placed under the tailor, who lives in the house; and we expect other tradesmen, as a shoemaker, carpenter &c. to which others are to be bound.

As the grace of God appears in any, together with suitable abilities, they are to be bred to the ministry, and we have already one or two in view for that purpose.

At ten they go to school, some to writing, some to reading. At present there are two masters and one mistress, who in teaching them to read the scripture, at the same time explain it to them, and sing and pray with them more or less as they think fit, not by form, but out of their own hearts, whereby they teach both themselves and children much knowledge in the scriptures, exercise their talents and build each other up in our most holy faith.

At noon we go to dinner all in the same room, and between that and two o'clock every one is employed in something useful, but no time is allowed for idleness or play, which are Satan's darling hours to tempt children to all manner of wickedness, as lying, cursing, swearing, uncleanness &c., so that though we are about seventy in family yet we hear no more noise than if it was a private house.

From 2 'till 4 they go again to school, as in the morning, and from 4 to 6 to work in their respective stations as before mentioned. At six the children go to supper, when the master and mistresses attend to help them, and sing with them, and watch over their words and actions.

At seven the family all goes to church, where is a psalm sung and exposition after the second lesson, as in the morning service. And at our return about 8 many of the parishioners come in to hear Mr. Whitefield examine and instruct the children by way of question and answer, which perhaps is as edifying to all present, as any of his sermons or expositions. His main business is to ground the children in their belief of original sin, and to make them sensible of their damnable state by nature, and the absolute necessity of a change to be wrought on their souls by the power of God, before they can be in a salvable state, or have any real right to call themselves Christians; for this purpose they are ordered to get by heart the excellent articles of *Original Sin,* of *Free Will* and of *Justification.*

At nine o'clock... the children [go] up to their bedroom, where some person commonly sings and prays again with them. Before they go to bed, each boy, as in the morning, is seen to kneel by his bedside, and is ordered to pray from his own heart for a quarter of an hour, some person instructing them how to pray...

On the Lord's Day we all dine on cold meat, prepared the day before, because all may attend the worship of God, which we have that day four times at church, which fills those hours employed at work on the other days. And thus is our time all laid out in the service of God, the variety of which is a sufficient relaxation to a well-disposed mind and obviates idle pretenses for what is called innocent (though in reality damnable) recreations...⁷

Highlanders defeated at Mosa: June 15, 1740

When William McIntosh was 14 years old he went off to war with his father Captain John Mackintosh Mor, the leader of Scots Highlanders who had founded Darien, Georgia.

In 1740 war was brewing between England and Spain and spilling over into the Spanish colony of Florida and the English colonies of South Carolina and Georgia. General James Oglethorpe, the commander of English forces in South Carolina and Georgia, was preparing to attack the Spanish stronghold at St. Augustine. The invasion would be supported by a fleet of British vessels: five ships were assigned to blockade St. Augustine and several privateers were authorized to plunder the Spaniards.

In *British Drums on the Southern Frontier*, Larry Ivers describes the preparations for war:

> On 2 May, Oglethorpe ordered John Mackintosh, commonly called John Mohr (Big John), the forty-year-old commander of the Darien militia, to recruit the Highland Independent Company of Foot. Captain Mackintosh returned to Darien from Frederica on 6 May and recruited his company of warlike Highlanders within about five hours. The company was authorized 115 officers and men, but only 70 men could be recruited; there were not enough Highland men to fill up a 35-man ranger troop, a 115-man foot company, and still have enough left to protect the women and children of Darien. The men of the Highland Independent Company of Foot were dressed and armed in the Highland fashion. Their skirt-like

plaids were wool tartans about ten to twelve yards long, part of which was gathered and belted around the waist, making a knee-length kilt. The remainder of the material was draped over the left shoulder and fastened with a brooch. It was a practical garment that also served as a blanket. Some of the men probably wore little kilts (similar to modern kilts). Scotch plaids were sold in the trustees' store and seem not to have been any particular pattern.[8]

Oglethorpe assigned four hundred soldiers of the 42nd Regiment stationed at Frederica to prepare to invade Florida, while the rest of the regiment remained on garrison duty at forts and outposts along the coastal frontier. About two hundred Indians agreed to accompany the British troops.

Oglethorpe moved south of the St. Johns River with an advance party and captured Fort Diego, a fortified plantation house belonging to a Spanish colonist. The Highlanders, meanwhile, were on their way to join Oglethorpe. Local historian Bessie Lewis picks up the story:

> Soon the Highland Company, with some of the Indians, were marching from Darien up the River Road toward the pass where later Fort Barrington would be built. There they would cross the Altamaha and go on to join the regiment.
>
> Young William McIntosh, son of Captain John McIntosh Mohr, was with them. He had run away from home and was with the Indians, who would keep him hidden from his father until they crossed the Altamaha, when it would be too late to send him back to Darien.[9]

The source of this story was presumably William himself, because his grandson Thomas Spalding would later write this version of it:

> William McIntosh, the eldest son of John More McIntosh, named after his grand-uncle, Brigadier General William McIntosh, who commanded the Highlanders in the rising of 1715, was not quite fourteen years of age when his father marched from Darien. He wished to accompany his father, but was refused. He pursued the moving columns, and overtook them at Barrington. His father sent him back the next day with an armed guard. He then took a small boat and passed up to Clarke's bluff, on the south side of the Altamaha. He intended to keep in the rear until the troops had crossed the St. Mary's river. He soon fell in with seven Indians who knew him (for Darien was then the great rendezvous of the Indians) and he had acquired something of their language. The Indians were greatly attached to the Highlanders, not only as being the soldiers of their beloved man, General Oglethorpe, but because of their wild manners, of their manly sports, of their eastern costume, so much resembling their own. The young soldier was received and caressed by them. They entered into all his views. Following after the advancing troops, they told him every thing that passed in the white man's camp; but carefully concealed his presence among them, until after the passage of the St. Mary's, when, with much triumph they led him to his father, and said, "that he was a young warrior, and would fight; that the great Spirit would watch over his life, for he loved young warriors."[10]

The Highlanders, the 42nd Regiment, and troops from South Carolina joined Oglethorpe's advance party on the south bank of the St. Johns River on May 15. Ivers picks up the story:

> In the cool of that evening Oglethorpe set out with a detachment of rangers and the Highland Company to resupply his garrison at Fort Diego seventeen miles to the south-southeast. The following morning, as the tired soldiers pulled the supply carts within sight of Fort Diego, an ambush was suddenly triggered by a party of Yemassee Indians. Gabriel Baugh, a Salzburger serving as an English Ranger and one of Oglethorpe's servant-bodyguards, was immediately killed. The Spanish allied Indians took advantage of the confusion to cut off Baugh's head and escape through the woods. Oglethorpe began an immediate pursuit of the Yemassee toward Saint Augustine through thickets and swamps. The regulars and Highlanders probably fell behind, but Oglethorpe and his rangers continued a hot pursuit on horseback for several miles, causing the Indians to drop Baugh's head. During the chase Oglethorpe had a horse shot from under him and his coat was reportedly torn by the Indians' musket balls. That night the weary pursuers returned to Fort Diego, having rounded up thirty badly needed Spanish horses. The most effective result of the pursuit was the Yemassee Indians' refusal to ambush Oglethorpe again.[11]

Oglethorpe and his detachment of rangers and Highlanders returned to the main camp on the St. Johns River, and he continued to plan an attack on St. Augustine. Ivers explains that Oglethorpe did not plan to lay siege to St. Augustine; he planned to capture the town by an assault of land forces and naval forces. Once he had captured the town, he planned an artillery bombardment against Castillo de San Marcos, the Spanish stronghold at St. Augustine.

The invasion force moved to Fort Diego on May 20. Oglethorpe and some of his officers, escorted by a detachment of the Highland Company and some Indian allies, explored the coast around St. Augustine. "Oglethorpe and his officers," Ivers reports, "set such a fast pace that the independently minded Indians and the already tired Highlanders, on foot, dropped behind. ...long, fast marches through deep sand under a hot sun with full equipment is extremely exhausting... and death by sunstroke was not uncommon during the campaign."[12]

In early June, Oglethorpe placed the South Carolina Regiment, a detachment of the 42nd Regiment, and an artillery battery on a peninsula on the north side of the harbor at St. Augustine. Oglethorpe led two hundred soldiers, two hundred seamen and about two hundred Indians to capture Anastasia Island on the south side of the harbor.

To keep the Spaniards in St. Augustine from foraging for food and gathering cattle, Oglethorpe established a force to patrol the mainland north of the Spanish town. Ivers tells the story:

> On 9 June, Oglethorpe assembled the flying party and gave its officers their orders. The Troop of Highland Rangers, commanded by Captain Hugh Mackay, Jr., took ten men on the mission, half of whom were officers. The Troop of English Rangers, under Lieutenant Robert Scroggs, counted only eight men... The Troop of Carolina Rangers, composed of South Carolina volunteers... mustered nine men. This troop, com-

manded by Captain William Palmer, had been formed after landing in Florida. The Highland Independent Company of Foot, under Captain John Mackintosh, included only fifty-seven men since several were sick and left behind. Thirty Uchee Indians served under a white trader named James Hewit, and ten Yamacraw and Creek followed the leadership of the half-Indian, Thomas Jones... In order to provide a disciplined core around which the party could be bolstered during battle, a regular red-coated detachment including a sergeant and twelve privates was added from the Forty-second Regiment of Food. The entire flying party apparently consisted of 137 men of all ranks.

Oglethorpe gave the ill-defined operational control of the party to Colonel John Palmer... but actual command of the soldiers was retained by Captain Mackay.

...The flying party left Fort Diego on 10 June and marched to a place between Saint Augustine and Fort Diego called the "Grove," where they camped the first night. They arrived at Fort Mosa about noon the following day. The fortification was described as "four Square with a Flanker at each Corner, banked round with Earth, having a Ditch without on all Sides lined round with prickly Palmetto Royal and... a Well and House within, and a Look Out." The British had partially demolished the structure during their previous visit a few days before. The gate had been carried off, a large breach had been battered in each of two walls, and the house within had been burned, making the structure no longer useful as a fortification.

General Oglethorpe had instructed the flying party to range west and east across the narrow strip of land between the Diego and Saint John Rivers, taking advantage of their mobility... They were to spend no more than one night in any one location, hiding in the thickets by night and moving into the open during the day to intercept Spanish foraging parties... Nevertheless, most of the officers chose to ignore the general's instructions by establishing a semipermanent camp at demolished Fort Mosa.

...On Saturday, 14 June, three hundred Spanish infantry, dragoons, militia, and Yemassee Indians were assembled and briefed. Captain Antonio Salgado was appointed as the commander and ordered to conduct a predawn assault.

At about eleven o'clock that night the Spanish raiding force quietly moved out of Fort San Marcos and began a cautious advance toward the sleeping camp. The ranger patrol and the Spanish raiders apparently missed making contact by only a few minutes. Salgado's force arrived near Fort Mosa at about two o'clock on Sunday morning, 15 June. A small reconnaissance party was sent forward to ascertain the positions of the British, and the dragoons were dispatched in a half circle around the fort to station themselves astride the route of escape to Fort Diego. An hour later the reconnaissance party returned with information concerning the British positions and strength. Their details of the British flying party's unpreparedness bolstered Spanish confidence.

About three o'clock, when Colonel Palmer had the drums "beat to arms," the majority of the Carolina and British Rangers left their blankets and dressed. Palmer then walked into the fort and found most of the soldiers asleep. After he berated them for their laziness and inefficiency nearly all got up and dressed; however after standing to arms for a few minutes most of the soldiers within the fort and some of those outside crawled back into their bedrolls.

Captain Salgado's soldiers deserve praise for their stealth and discipline. They were divided into three parties and apparently attacked from as many directions. They were able to move unseen to within almost one hundred yards of the fort before one of the sentries, a Carolina Ranger, discovered them moving forward in the first light of dawn. The frightened sentry ran back to the fort crying that the Spaniards were upon them.

Colonel Palmer and Thomas Jones were standing in the gateway talking when they heard the sentry's warning. Palmer immediately called for everyone to stand to their arms and to hold their fire until the Spaniards had fired first. No sooner had he spoken than a detachment of the Highlanders stationed in the nearest bastion opened fire. With curses Palmer ordered the Carolina and English Rangers into the moat. The Spaniards began pouring volleys on the fort.

Jones ran inside to assemble his Indians who were just waking from a sound sleep. He found the entire party in a state of confusion. Half-dressed soldiers were searching frantically for weapons. Shouting officers and sergeants were vainly trying to gather their men in their appointed bastions.

Captain Mackay had probably been wakened by the commotion. He was dressed only in a shirt, a pair of linen breeches, [and] stockings, and was carrying a small sword and a musket. Mackay ordered the officer of the guard, Cornet Baillie, to defend the gate with his guard of eighteen men, but within a short time the Spaniards began pushing them back. Mackay then ordered his cousin, Ensign Charles Mackay of the Highland Company, to support the guard with twelve men.

Outside in the moat the rangers were holding their own. Lieutenant Scroggs and the English Rangers were separated from Captain Palmer's Carolina troop. Captain Palmer had just finished pulling his boots on and buckling his spurs when he heard the warning shouts. He grabbed his brother and another ranger and ran to the moat about twelve yards away, believing they were in more danger from the Highlanders' fire to the rear than from the Spaniards' fire to the front. A short distance away Colonel Palmer, William Steads, and another ranger kept firing at the Spanish party that was trying to enter the gate. The rangers outside the fort do not appear to have been in much danger at that moment; the Spaniards were more interested in getting inside.

Inside the fort Captain Mackay and Jones met while moving from bastion to bastion, each trying to rally the men and improve their dispositions. Jones reported he had killed the Spanish officer who had led the first assault. He suggested that Mackay reinforce those Highlanders who were trying to hold the gate.

The Highlanders repulsed the first two charges, but a considerable body of Spaniards finally forced their way in by sheer weight of numbers. Captain Mackay hurriedly dispatched what men he could find to reinforce the gate, but it was too late. The fighting became hand to hand. The Spaniards had the advantage in that their numbers were greater and they were using bayonets to cut the British to pieces. The Highlanders had left their bayonets and targets (shields) behind to make them lighter on foot. Without a target a broad-swordsman was no match for a trained soldier with a bayonet. They began to give way. The Spaniards from the other two assault parties were now hacking their way into the fort through the two breaches in the walls.

Colonel Palmer was loading his gun when he was hit by a musket ball. Bleeding at the mouth, he finished loading his gun and died.[13]

Among the Highlanders at Mosa was Roderick "Rory" McIntosh, a grandson of Brigadier William Mackintosh of Borlum. "I am a scoundrel, sir," he told a military officer decades later. "At Musa, a Captain of the Spanish Grenadiers was charging at the head of his company, and, like a vermint, sir, I lay in the bushes, and shot the gallant fellow."[14]

Although "the Highlanders and Indians fought bravely," local historian Bessie Lewis writes, "there was no hope from the first. Many were killed, others were captured, only a few survived. Young William McIntosh, fighting like the soldier he was, saw his father wounded and captured by the Spaniards. Among others taken prisoner that day were Ranald MacDonald, Joseph Burges, Alexander Cameron and John Mackintosh Bain. James Mackay was among those who were killed."[15]

John Mackintosh Mor described the battle in a letter to Alexander Mackintosh, a merchant in Lothbury:

...about an hour before day light, we were Attacted by Seven hundred of the Enemy, as we were Credibly Inform'd afterwards, where they met with as Hot a Reception as might possibly be Expected from So Small a Party against Such a Number, keeping a Closs fire uppon them for about an hour, and afterwards Attacting them Sword in hand – Where we hade the Misfortune being overpower'd by Numbers, to be Cut to pieces; Twenty Eight of us taken prisoners, If any Escaped it is more than I Can tell, but My Self a Cornet, and Quartermaster belonging to Capt. Mckays Troop was Stript of our Cloaths, our hands bound behind our backs And So Carried in Captives to the Town, where we Remaind in Confinement four Months, dureing Which time we were Civily us'd by the Governour of Said town...[16]

Military historian Larry Ivers continues his account of the Battle of Mosa:

Two thirds of the men of the Highland Company were casualties. The detachment of regulars were all dead, wounded, or captured. Almost half of the Highland Rangers had been killed or taken prisoner. One fourth of the English Rangers were dead. The majority of the Yamacraw and Creek were dead or captured.

Captain Mackay scrambled to the top of the earthen wall and called to those below to follow. He and William Mackintosh, the fourteen-year-old son of Captain Mackintosh, jumped off the wall into the moat below.

Shortly afterwards Jones and everyone who was able also climbed over the wall. Jones met Captain Palmer and his brother near the moat and, in the company of six Indians, they began to force their way through the Spaniards under the cover of thick clouds of gunsmoke. A Yemassee Indian lunged at Jones, but Captain Palmer turned and shot him. Jones and Palmer broke through and ran to the stream near the fort, wading down to its junction with the Diego River where they met Captain Mackay, Lieutenant Scroggs, and the men they had been able to bring from the fort. The appearance of Scroggs suggests that he had also been caught napping. He wore only a shirt and was armed only with a pistol. Mackay had a wound across two fingers and two other wounds, "in his Breech and the Top of his Yard." He said he had been wounded while defending the gate, but the Carolina officers suspected he must have received his wounds from the prickly palmetto royal that had been planted in the moat around the fort.[17]

Thomas Spalding describes his grandfather William McIntosh's escape from the deathtrap at Mosa:

He followed his father's footsteps until he saw him fall, covered with many wounds, at fort Moosa. But the great Spirit did watch over him most miraculously. For when he saw his father fall, he was so transfixed with horror, that not until a Spanish officer laid hold upon his plaid, was he roused to action. Light and elastic as a steel bow, he slipped from under the grasp of this officer, and made his escape with the wreck of the corps. It was from the lips of this gentleman (my aged grandfather) I learned much of what I know respecting General Oglethorpe, and the times and the things of that day.[18]

Ivers describes the aftermath of the battle:

The remains of the party were in a perilous state. At any moment the Spaniards might find them and add them to the list of casualties. One man was ordered to swim across the river to Point Quartell and ask Colonel Vanderhussen to send over a boat. A short time later the scout boat *Georgia* was sighted coming down the river. The boat was hailed and twenty-five thankful survivors boarded and were taken to Point Quartell and safety. Other survivors made their way to safety by ones and twos.

At Fort Mosa, the Spaniards were surveying their victory in the early Sunday morning sunlight. Their prisoners included Captain Mackintosh and about a dozen men of the Highland Independent Company, Cornet Baillie and Quartermaster McQueen of the Highland Rangers, four or five men of the Forty-second Regiment, and an unknown number of Indians. The Spaniards stripped them, bound their hands behind their backs, and began marching them to Saint Augustine. Two prisoners who were too badly wounded to walk were killed and their heads and genitals were chopped off. One of the severed, dripping heads was sadistically rubbed in the face of Edward Lyng, a soldier of the Forty-second Regiment. A total of sixty-three British dead, including both whites and Indians, were left lying in and around the fort. Determining Spanish casualties is difficult. British estimates placed Spanish losses at between sixteen and three hundred. Governor Montiano admitted to losing ten men.[19]

The loss at Mosa thwarted Oglethorpe's strategy for capturing St. Augustine, and on July 4 he called off the attack. The results of the battle, however, did not shake his faith in Highlanders as warriors. "The Georgia Rangers, the Highlanders and some of the Creek Indians had but too fatal an occasion of giving proofs of their resolution at Moosa," Oglethorpe wrote, "where most of those who died fought with an obstinacy worthy of the Greeks or Romans."[20]

John Mackintosh Mor's role in the war on the southern frontier ended abruptly in defeat and imprisonment, eerily similar to his fate in the Jacobite Rising of 1715. By 1740, he had much more to lose. He was a husband and a father. He had established himself as a high-ranking gentleman in Scotland and he had become the leader of a strategically important settlement in the New World. When he was captured at Mosa he was cut off from everything he cherished and he could only wonder what would become of his family, the settlement at Darien, and his own future.

Darien dwindles after Highlanders defeated

Bessie Lewis describes the aftermath of the ill-fated offensive at St. Augustine and the disaster at Mosa:

> The invasion failed, and the town of Darien bore the greatest loss. The bagpipes skirled the clan dirges as the men came up the river to Darien to tell the widows and orphans the sad news. Most of them expecting the Spaniards to invade the frontier, fled to Fort Argyle [between Darien and Savannah] and some obtained shelter in the orphanage.
>
> So many Highlanders had died in the battle; their leader, John McIntosh Mohr, was in a Spanish prison with his comrades. The fields at Darien lay fallow, black cattle ran wild, the pit saws were idle – the servants who would have attended to these matters of every day living were manning the scout boats or in the regiment of the Rangers, patrolling the woods or training for the invasion that was daily expected.

The women and children were afraid to come home – there were those who said the Scottish town of Darien was dead, that it would never recover.[21]

John Mackintosh Mor's family seeks refuge

After John Mackintosh Mor was taken prisoner his family was fragmented. His 14-year-old son William, who had escaped from Mosa, joined Oglethorpe's regiment at Frederica across the marsh from Darien. John Mor's 13-year-old son Lachlan and daughter Ann, who was no older than 3, remained in the orphanage at Bethesda near Savannah.[22]

"The Spirit of the Lord I hope is beginning to blow among the dry bones here," Lachlan wrote while staying at Bethesda. "The House was never since I came thither likelier to answer to the end of its Institution than now: Little Boys and Little Girls, at this and that corner, crying unto the Lord, that he would have Mercy upon them."[23]

John Mackintosh Mor's wife Marjory took the other children – John, age 12, Phineas, 8, and George, less than a year old – to the fort at Palachacola on the South Carolina side of the Savannah River. Marjory sought refuge with her husband's distant kinsman John Mackintosh, who had been given command of the fort when his brother Aeneas had returned to Scotland to inherit the position of Chief of Clan Mackintosh.

Marjory Mackintosh also received protection and sustenance from William Stephens, the secretary to the Georgia Trustees.[24]

Oglethorpe suffers

Larry Ivers describes the physical and psychological effect of the failure of the Florida invasion on General James Oglethorpe:

During August and September 1740 General Oglethorpe isolated himself in his house at Frederica. Long marches, lack of sleep, bad water, and tainted food had sickened him. His most serious illness, however, resulted from the psychological shock that his extraordinary pride and self-confidence had suffered because of his defeat in Florida.

About October, Oglethorpe overcame his fever and the shame of his failure and began thinking about his responsibilities to Georgia. During the following twenty-one months he worked unceasingly to bolster Georgia's defenses with the knowledge that Florida's Governor Montiano would invade Georgia and South Carolina as soon as he could amass enough men and ships.[25]

Benjamin Mackintosh goes to Charleston

Some of the Highlanders who had founded Darien relocated to Charleston to seek their fortunes. By moving to South Carolina they escaped the Georgia Trustees' policies restricting land ownership and prohibiting slavery. John Mackintosh of Holmes and Benjamin Mackintosh – a natural son of Brigadier William Mackintosh of Borlum – moved to Charleston in October of 1740.

Lachlan McGillivray, a young settler at Darien who had learned the language of the Creek Indians, went to Charleston in 1740 to work in an Indian trading company operated by Archibald McGillivray.

John McLeod, the Presbyterian minister at Darien, moved to South Carolina to serve as the pastor of a church on Edisto Island not far south of Charleston.[26]

John Mackintosh Mor languishes in prison

At that time both John Mackintosh Mor and his uncle Brigadier William Mackintosh of Borlum were imprisoned due to military misfortune but their circumstances were different. The Brigadier was more than 70 years old and passed his time in Edinburgh Castle writing learned treatises. John Mackintosh Mor was about 40 years old and languished in a jail cell in Spain worrying about his wife and young children.

After the Battle of Mosa on the American frontier between British colonies and Spanish colonies, the victorious Spaniards took John Mackintosh Mor and their other prisoners to their stronghold at St. Augustine. Then they transferred him to Havana, and later transferred him to Spain.

He wrote a letter dated May 1, 1741, and signed "John Mackintosh Moore" asking Alexander Mackintosh, a merchant in Lothbury, to provide credit for obtaining food, clothing, and other necessities while he was imprisoned.[27]

Afraid that the first letter may not have been delivered, he sent a second letter dated June 20, 1741. Emphasizing his clan connection with Alexander Mackintosh, he reported that he had no way of knowing what had become of his wife or children; he was not even aware that his eldest son William had escaped from the battlefield of Mosa. He wrote:

> Sir
> You being my Friend and Namesake, staying nigh the Court makes me presume to write you in my Necessity. That you may know who gives you this Trouble, my name is John Mcintosh Son to Lachlan Mcintosh who was Brother to Brigadier Mcintosh of Borlom. Now I will inform you what my case is

and how I came here, no doubt you have heard of General Oglethorpe's disappointment at Florida and how the Highlanders were cut to pieces except a few had the bad fortune to be taken Prisoners, of which number I was one, and what compleats our Misery and makes it worse than others of his Brittanick Majesty's Subjects is that we were never enquired for, by any person what came of us, nor do I know whom to apply to. I had the Command of the above Highlanders since their Settlement in Georgia. When the War began the General sent for me and presented me with a Captains Commission, told me he had Authority to raise Troops and that my Company should be independent under the Kings Pay. With that encouragement and all of us being willing and forward to serve our King and Country, I listed Seventy Men, all in Highland Dress, marched to the Siege, was ordered to scout nigh Augustine and molest the Enemy while the General and the rest of his little army went to an Island where we could have no succour of them. I punctually obeyed my orders untill Seven Hundred Spaniards sallied out from the Garrison one hour before day light, they did not surprise us for we were all under arms ready to receive them, which we did briskly, keeping a constant firing for a quarter of an hour, when they prest on us with numbers was obliged to take our Swords, untill the most of us was shot and cut to pieces. You are to observe we had but Eighty Men, and the engagement was in view of the rest of our Army, but could not come to our assistance by being in the 'foresaid Island under the Enemy's Guns. They had Twenty Prisoners, a few got off, the rest killed As we were well informed by some of themselves they had 300d. killed on the spot besides several wounded. We were all stripp't naked of

Cloaths, brought to Augustine where we remained three months in close confinement, afterwards sent to the Havannah, where the Governor was so civil to all called Officers, that we had the Liberty of the City for our confinement. After staying three months here, was ordered on board a Ship for St. Sebastians in old Spain. Tho' the Havannah Governor recommended me as Captain of foot, my treatment was to be put in close confinement in the Common Town Jayl, and my Allowance Bread and Water. If it was not for six pence a day his Brittanick Majesty allows all Prisoners we might starve. You are to know I left a Wife and seven Children in Georgia for ought I know starving there for all my Servants was listed to make up the Company. There is a son of Corebrough Mcqueens and a Nephew of Duncan's here who was an Ensign in a troop of Rangers belonging to the Trustees As also one Mcdonald who has a Family in Georgia. I hope when this comes to hand as there is a great many Spanish Prisoners in England, by your endeavors you'll get some of them to be exchanged for us four, if not a little Credit to help us in Cloaths and a better living which we want much. In Justice and for the Credit of the Country I ought to be maintained conformed to the Station I am Prisoner. I do not doubt your Diligence in applying the proper persons whom I believe to be the Secretary of War and the Trustees. I wrote to them both but no Answer, begs pardon for this Trouble...[28]

While imprisoned in Spain, John Mackintosh Mor sent at least two letters to an official with the Georgia Trustees. He wrote on June 24, 1741:

... We were sent... to this place to our Misery. ...to be confined in the common Jayl and allowed no more than bread and water. I thought proper to acquaint you with this that it might be made Publick. The reason I trouble you is, the little correspondence I had with You by writing when at Darien. And what Compleats my Misfortune and makes it really worse than any other of his Brittanick Majesty's Subjects is, that there was no Inquiry made concerning me whether Dead of Alive, nor do I know whom to apply to, therefore I expect you'll please be so good as to Inquire and apply to the proper persons for my Releasement and a little Credit to my self, and the other two Gentlemen who has served the Trustees in the Troop of Rangers these five Years, to support us in our Necessitys here, I having faithfully Served the Honble. the Trustees for five Years, besides the Love I had for my King and Country made me forsake my Wife and Children and all my Effects, so that now I hope by your good Endeavors in Representing my case I shall have no reason to complain if God spares me to see England. I am

Sir with great Esteem

Your most Obedient humble Servt.

John Mackintosh Moore[29]

New settlers arrive at Darien

To revive depopulated Darien, the Georgia Trustees conducted another recruiting drive in the Scottish Highlands. Captain Hugh Mackay played a major role in the recruitment effort, historian Anthony Parker points out: "Of the forty-three emigrants from the Highlands, twelve were surnamed Mackay and two other men, who had families, were connected directly to the Mackay clan through marriage. Almost half the new emigrants were known Mackays and the other names represented included MacDonald, Munroe, Douglas and Grant."[30] The new settlers arrived at Darien in December of 1741.

Lachlan McIntosh joins the Frederica regiment

Lachlan McIntosh, who had lived in the orphanage at Bethesda since February of 1740, left the orphanage on April 26, 1742. Lachlan, who had turned age 15 in March, "Was ordered by Gen. Oglethorpe to his regiment at Frederica, being a cadet there." Lachlan's duties with the regiment included standing guard and herding cattle, but he apparently did not engage in combat. At Frederica, Lachlan reunited with his brother William, age 16, who had been taken into the regiment after the Highland Company was decimated at Mosa, where William escaped after seeing his father taken prisoner.[31]

Spaniards invade Georgia: May-July, 1742

The King of Spain ordered forces from Cuba and Florida to attack South Carolina and Georgia in the spring of 1742. Nearly two thousand infantrymen, dragoons, artillery gunners and scouts, including sixty Indians, sailed from St. Augustine to the Georgia coast on a fleet of fifty-two vessels. The British defensive force under General James Oglethorpe consisted of fewer than a thousand men stationed at posts along the coast supported by an inadequate amount of artillery. As the Spanish fleet approached, British recruiters sought volunteers in Savannah. The Highland Independent Company of Foot at Darien – commanded by Lieutenant Charles Mackay while John Mackintosh Mor was a prisoner of war in Spain – was ordered to join Oglethorpe's forces at St. Simons Island. The Troop of Highland Rangers commanded by Captain Hugh Mackay, Jr., also reported for duty at St. Simons. Small parties of Chickasaw, Creek, and Yamacraw Indians came to support their friend Oglethorpe. By the time the Spanish fleet anchored at the mouth of St. Simons Sound, about five hundred British soldiers had assembled on St. Simons Island.[32]

On July 5 the Spanish fleet forced past the guns of small British vessels and the artillery of Fort St. Simons on the south end of St. Simons Island. Once the fleet entered the Frederica River, about fifteen hundred Spanish soldiers conducted an assault landing throughout the evening and the night, sweeping aside resistance from Georgia Rangers and their Indian allies. British troops abandoned Fort St. Simons and began marching after midnight along the trail to Frederica on the north end of the island.[33]

"On the Georgia mainland the settlers panicked" Ivers reports. "Women and children fled from Darien to Fort Argyle [between Darien and Savannah] and beyond, while those from Savannah hastily sought refuge in Abercorn and other outlying settlements in an attempt to somehow evade the rape and pillage that they believed was imminent. Fear was only slightly less prevalent in South Carolina, for the real prize for any enemy fleet would have been the sacking of Charles Town."[34]

British rangers patrolling the trail to Frederica encountered a Spanish reconnaissance party on July 7. The rangers raced to Frederica to inform Oglethorpe, who decided to attack the Spaniards while they were confined on the narrow trail through the semitropical forest. Ivers describes the encounter:

> The Highland Company, mustering between thirty and forty men, was the only infantry unit in formation prepared to

march. Oglethorpe commandeered a horse and began leading the Highlanders out of the town gate and down the trail at a run. He was quickly joined by Captain Thomas Jones with his rangers, Toonahowi and a party of Yamacraw and Creek, Lieutenant Scroggs and a detachment of English Rangers, and Captain William Gray of South Carolina with a party of Squirrel King's Chickasaw from near Augusta. Running a long distance on a July day in Georgia is exhausting, especially if you are carrying about twenty-five pounds of weapons and equipment; nevertheless, six Highlanders and most of the Indians managed to keep up with the galloping rangers.

About a mile southeast of Frederica, as the disordered body of provincials and Indians rounded a slight bend in the wood-enclosed trail, they saw the Spaniards' lead element on the other side of a small open savannah to their front. Captain Sanchez was moving his reconnoitering party toward a nearby creek bed that he intended to use as a defensive position. Without hesitating, Oglethorpe spurred his horse toward them. For the Chickasaw, Yamacraw, Creek and Highlanders, all warlike by tradition, the charge represented life at its best. If the rangers felt the rising temperature of fear they had little time to reflect upon it; they swept the lead element aside and collided with the main body of Spanish regulars, scouts, and Indians. Oglethorpe and his followers never relinquished the momentum they gained from their surprising charge. Two Spaniards threw down their weapons and surrendered to Oglethorpe who was at the head of his men. Toonahowi, wounded in his right arm, drew a pistol with his left hand and killed a Spanish officer who was threatening him. Lieutenant Scroggs plunged his horse into the milling Spaniards and forced the surrender of their commander, Captain Sanchez. Captain Hernandez was captured shortly afterward. The Spaniards' resistance disintegrated and they began stumbling wildly into the woods and back along the trail. Oglethorpe and the rangers pursued a party of fleeing Spaniards about three and a half miles before calling a halt to wait for Mackay's Highlanders and Demere's regulars to catch up. The Creek, Chickasaw, some Highlanders, and a few rangers remained near the battle site, running down the terrified survivors. The Spaniards suffered thirty-six men killed, captured, or missing, and most of the remainder were temporarily lost in the woods and thickets. The British lost one man, a Highlander, from heat exhaustion.[35]

A ranger serving with Oglethorpe identified the Highlander who died from heat exhaustion: "Mr. Maclane a Highland Gentleman who running very hard in pursuit of the Enemy spoiled the Circulation of his Blood and died Soon after he was brought to Town."[36]

The Battle of Bloody Marsh: July 7, 1742

Soldiers from the regiment at Frederica went out to support the Highlanders, rangers and Indians led by General Oglethorpe who had driven off a Spanish reconnaissance party. Expecting a counter-attack, Oglethorpe posted the combined force to guard the trail leading to Frederica.[37] Ivers describes the situation:

The position Oglethorpe selected to block the trail was between four and a half and five miles south-southeast of Frederica on the western edge of present Bloody Marsh. He placed Captain Demere and his company of about sixty regulars, who had just arrived from Frederica, on the left (east) side of the trail and the Highland Company and the rangers, about forty-five to fifty men, on the right (west) side. A branch of Bloody Marsh, an open savannah perhaps a hundred yards wide, lay perpendicular to their front (south). The trail crossed this spongy marsh on a narrow causeway of brush and logs and led into the dense woods between the British positions. While Oglethorpe returned to Frederica the regulars and provincials prepared their blocking position by building several small piles of fallen logs and limbs in the tree line as protection from Spanish musket balls.

Meanwhile, a few Spaniards of the defeated reconnoitering party arrived at Fort Saint Simons about noon and reported the clash. Montiano reacted quickly by ordering Captain Antonio Barba to take three companies of grenadiers, probably between 150 and 200 men, and march to the battle site in order to protect the withdrawal of the members of the reconnoitering party, most of whom were scattered in the dense woods. The relief force set out and began picking up stragglers from the reconnoitering party as they marched north. Clouds had been gathering and now a light steady rain began to fall.

About three o'clock in the afternoon Captain Barba's grenadiers began crossing a narrow causeway spanning a marsh. A few survivors of the defunct reconnoitering party, who were acting as guides, noticed some piles of brush and logs situated in the woods on the far side of the marsh which they could not remember having seen before. Barba called a halt and sent a few men forward to investigate. When they drew near the far side of the marsh the brush and trees on both sides of the trail suddenly erupted with the blasts and smoke from dozens of muskets. Several Spaniards were cut down while running to the rear. Barba formed his three companies inside the cover of the trees on the south side of the marsh and began placing a disciplined fire on the British positions. A steady drizzle of rain held the smoke close to the ground, obscuring the scene. The Spaniards were shouting and their drummers were loudly beating Barba's commands. Demere's regulars became excited and a few turned and fled. They were soon followed by some more. Finally, three whole platoons broke and ran along with Captain Demere and another officer.

At Frederica, Oglethorpe... heard the distant firing. After ordering the units to follow, he spurred his horse toward the battle. About two miles north of the marsh he met Captain Demere and the three fugitive platoons who informed him that the entire force had been routed; however, Oglethorpe could still hear the firing and ordered them to return with him to the marsh...

Half of the British force had held courageously. To the left of the trail Lieutenant Patrick Sutherland and Sergeant John Stewart of Demere's company had somehow managed to hold a platoon of about fifteen men in place. To the right Lieutenant Charles Mackay's Highland Company and the rangers seem not to have ever considered leaving the battle. For about an hour Sutherland's and Mackay's outnumbered soldiers continued firing steadily across the marsh at the Spanish grenadiers.

The Spaniards were unaware that almost half of the British force had fled. About four o'clock, after firing all their ammunition, Captain Barba formed the three companies into marching order and began an orderly retreat to Fort Saint Simons. They reported an officer and six men killed, probably in the first few seconds of the fight, and two wounded men had been captured.

The Spaniards had just completed their withdrawal when Oglethorpe arrived. His elation is easy to imagine, for if the entire British force had been routed the effect on the morale of both regulars and provincials could have been disastrous. Instead, the brave stand by the soldiers under Sutherland and Mackay made the Spaniards seem less ominous and gave Oglethorpe's army new-found courage.[38]

The British victory at Bloody Marsh contrasted sharply with the British defeat two years earlier at Fort Mosa, where some of the same Spanish military units had crushed some of the same British units, particularly the Highlanders. "We have some Satisfaction for the Blood at Mosa," Oglethorpe declared in a letter to a friend.[39]

A ranger serving with Oglethorpe recorded his somewhat mistaken impression of the battle:

> The Spaniards hearing of the Fate their first Party met with sent out another 300 Men under the Command of Don Antonio Barbara Captain of a Company of Grenadiers; about three o' th' Clock in the afternoon the Spaniards advanced up to the Place where we were Posted and some of them being Come within our Lines a Sharp Fire continued on all hands and betwixt both parties for some time. The Spaniards fell in great Numbers amongst which was Several Officers and also that Famous Captain of Grenadiers; the Number of the Spaniards

was so great and their Fire so brisk, that some Platoons of ours gave way and were Retiring in Confusion but the timely presence of the General prevented their Retiring far. He immediately ordered them to Rally, riding himself up to the Place where he found Lieutt Sutherland and Lieutt Charles Mackay with the Highlanders and Rangers had Entirely defeated the Spaniards.[40]

As a soldier in the Frederica regiment, William McIntosh may have been among the fifteen regulars who did not flee or he may have been among his fellow Highlanders. When he described the Battle of Bloody Marsh fifty years later to his grandson Thomas Spalding, William McIntosh did not let historical facts interfere with a good Celtic tale. He apparently blended several events from the Spanish invasion of Georgia into one story. And, as in all legends, his account combines elements of folklore with historical events. Describing the scene when Oglethorpe hurried from Frederica to the battleground, Spalding writes:

> ...at the last bend of the marshy way, a scene opened upon him, which his proudest expectations could not have looked for; a scene to himself of glory and security; to his enemy of shame and defeat.
>
> The last bend of the marsh was covered by two hundred grenadiers, who lay dead or dying upon the field, while not an enemy was in sight. All was still, save sometimes at intervals a Highland shout or an Indian yell proclaimed that another and another had been found and dragged from his covert. But how rose that shout, how rang that yell, when the actors stood around their chief to hail him victor of the day. And we have

seen the eye glisten, and the voice rise, fifty years afterwards as we fondly listened to the tale by one who had mingled in the strife and been partner in the scene.

But we will detail the little that remains to be told. While the troops were attacked in the wood by the Spanish forces from their camp, they were overwhelmed by superior numbers, and became, as is sometimes the case with even veteran troops, seized with a panic, lest the Spaniards, pushing on, should take possession of the defile, and cut off their retreat. They therefore made a precipitate retreat, the Highlanders following in the rear reluctantly. After passing through the defile Lieut. McKay communicated to his friend Lieut. Southerland (who commanded the rear guard of the retreating forces, composed also of Highlanders) the feelings of his corps, and they agreed to drop behind, and as soon as the whole had passed the defile, as there were no Spaniards in view, to return through the brush and take post at the two points of the crescent. Four Indians that were with them, and particularly attached to the corps, remained with them. They had just taken post and concealed themselves in the woods when the Spaniards, having made all their arrangements for an advance, their grenadier regiment, the *elite* of their troops, advanced into the defile, where, seeing in the foot-prints the rapid retreat of the broken troops, and observing that their right was covered by an open morass, and their left, as they supposed, by an impracticable wall of brush-wood, and a border of dry white sand, they stacked their arms and sat down to take the refreshment that had become necessary after having been under arms many hours, believing as they did that the contest for the day was over. Just at that moment, a Highland cap was raised at either point, and the scene of death began. All was terror – no resistance was made – sometimes they attempted to fly along the marsh. The pass was too narrow. They were met and slaughtered by the broad-sword. Those that did escape, had at last to make their way to and through the brushwood, where many wounded perished, and their bodies were only found when all that remained of them were their whitened bones.

The young soldier of Fort Moosa, just then sixteen years of age, was there. No shout rose higher, no sword waved quicker than his upon that day. But his heart was as soft as it was brave, and there was melancholy in his mood, when standing upon the ground and pointing to where the victor stood, and where the vanquished fell, he told to his daughter's son this tale of other times.[41]

Local historian Bessie Lewis uses details from Spalding's account in her vivid telling of the Battle of Bloody Marsh:

Taking a party of Indians, the Rangers and the Highland Company, and ordering the regiment to follow, Oglethorpe advanced to meet the enemy, coming upon them in the deepest part of the woods, where there was neither time nor room for battle formation. Claymores flashing, muskets spitting fire, the eerie battle cry of the Highlanders with the skirling of bagpipes mingled with the war whoop of the Indians while the Scots and redmen took vengeance for comrades who fell at Moosa. Rangers galloped to right and left, their muskets taking bitter toll of Spanish lives. Completely routed, the Spaniards fled in disorder, with the British forces in pursuit.

Oglethorpe halted his men on the edge of an open meadow or savannah. There he posted three platoons of the regiment with the company of Highland infantry. Completely hidden in the thick woods, these forces commanded a full view of the savannah over which any fresh Spanish forces must pass going from their camp to Frederica.

The trap worked. Three Spanish captains, with one hundred grenadiers and two hundred foot soldiers, besides Indians and Negroes, marched into the savannah. Without suspicion of ambush they advanced into the meadow, marching boldly to the rhythm of drums. They halted, stacked their arms and prepared to cook a meal.

Suddenly a horse gave a snort of fright. Pandemonium broke loose – the Spaniards ran to their arms and tried to form for action. The Highlanders and soldiers of the regiment, shooting from ambush, brought down man after man, while the desperate Spaniards, unable to see their targets and untrained in woods warfare, fired wildly with little effect. Spanish officers were killed and their men scattered in all directions.

The air was filled with the smoke of black powder, settling low in the rain, and two platoons of the regiment became confused and began to retreat. Oglethorpe, galloping his horse toward the noise of battle, met and stopped them. They reported the British forces routed and Lieutenant Sutherland killed. With the noise of the battle still going on, Oglethorpe could not believe this, and he ordered them back to the savannah. His report to the Trustees tells the story: "I found the Spaniards entirely routed by one Platoon of the Regiment under the command of Lieut. Sutherland and the Highland

Company under Lieut. Charles Mackay …An officer whom the Prisoners said was Capt. Don Antonio Barba was taken prisoner but desperately wounded, and two others were prisoners dead on the spot. Lieut. Sutherland, Lieut. Charles Mackay and Sergt. Stuart having distinguished themselves, I appointed Lieut. Sutherland Brigade Major and Sergt. Stuart Second Ensign."

The Battle of Bloody Marsh was over… [42]

The legend of Bloody Marsh became a staple in the bardic repertoire of descendants of Scottish Highlanders. In a presidential address to the St. Andrew's Society of Savannah in 1936, Alexander R. MacDonell told this version of the tale:

The highland soldier has always had a military character for valor. Taught to consider courage as the most honorable virtue, cowardice the most disgraceful feeling, he was ready to follow wherever honor and duty called him, and to devote himself to his native country and to his clan.

With such principles and regarding any disgrace he might bring on his clan and district as the cruelest misfortune, the highland private soldier had a peculiar motive to exertion, and he knew that every proof which he displayed, either of bravery or cowardice, would find its way to his native home, and that he had a separate and individual reputation to sustain, which would be reflected on his family and clan.

The character of ardor belongs to the highlander; he acts from internal sentiment and possesses a kind of honor which does not permit him to retire from a danger with a confession of inferiority. Close charge was his ancient mode of attack, and it is probably from the impression engrafted in his nature that he still sustains the approaching point of a naked weapon with a steadier eye than any other man in Europe.

...A famous English General once said that in all his experiences of war the Scotch soldier was the only one who did not flinch from an assault with cold steel, but that, on the contrary, the Scotch Highlander delighted in a close hand to hand conflict, a delight which must have been hereditary in his blood...

The youthful Scotch Highlander, his imagination fired by the martial reputation of his race, often burned with zeal to bear arms and fight shoulder to shoulder with the other members of his clan, and many instances of such youthful warriors are to be found in the records of those battles in which the Scotch clans engaged.

Young William MacIntosh presents a typical example of such warlike precocity. At the age of fourteen, desiring to join his father, John Mohr, in the invasion of Florida... he determined to follow anyhow... He followed his father until he saw him fall at Fort Moosa, covered with wounds...

...an armada of forty vessels and between three and four thousand troops from the West Indies engaged the defenses which Oglethorpe had thrown up, entered the inner passage and landed. A great crisis had come. For the Scotchmen, it was to be a great victory, a Bannockburn of the new world. The battle which ensued was known as the Battle of Bloody Marsh. It was one of the decisive battles of the world.

Carlisle said that half the world was hidden in embryo under it. The Yankee nation itself was involved, the greatest phenomenon of the ages.

Whitfield said that it determined that North America should be left to the exploitation of the Anglo-Saxon, the Celtic and the Teutonic. By it North America remained English instead of becoming Spanish.

The decisive blow of the battle was struck by the Highlanders under Lieuts. Sutherland and Mackay...

The Spaniards marched into the defile and, supposing the contest over for the day, stacked arms and began to partake of refreshments. Sutherland and Mackay, who, from their hiding places, had watched the movements of the Spaniards, now from either end of the line, raised the Highland shout and signaled the work of death to begin. Immediately, the Highlanders poured into the unsuspecting enemy a well delivered and most deadly fire. Volley succeeded volley and the sand was soon strewed with the dead and dying.

Terror and dismay seized the Spaniards, who, making no resistance, attempted to fly along the marsh. Discipline was gone; orders were unheeded; safety alone was sought; and when, with a Highland shout of triumph, the hidden foes burst among them, with level muskets and flashing claymoors, the panic stricken Spaniards fled in every direction; some to the marsh, where they were mired and taken; others along the defile, where they were met by the broad sword; and still others into the thicket, where they became undiscovered and perished; and only a few succeeded in escaping to their camp.

In these actions William MacIntosh, already mentioned, was conspicuous, although he was only sixteen years old at the time. No shout rose higher and no sword raised quicker than his on that day... He was avenging the capture of his father, John Mohr MacIntosh, by the Spaniards at Fort Moosa.[43]

Spanish invasion force withdraws

Late in the day of the Battle of Bloody Marsh, Oglethorpe led his army southward to within two miles of the Spanish army. The British army spent the night on the trail. The next morning, the British army marched back to Frederica while rangers and Indian allies stayed behind to harass the Spanish camp.[44]

One of the rangers reported an incident that may have contributed to the legend that the Spanish soldiers at Bloody Marsh had stopped to cook a meal: "The Spaniards after this never ventured out beyond their Centinels who were also Fortified. I having been out by order observing their Motions and within Musquet shot of them, The Rangers and Indians were always so near them that nine Spaniards were shot in their Camp as they were Eating."[45]

A few days after the battles on the trail, three Spanish vessels explored the Frederica River to see whether infantry and artillery could approach Fort Frederica by water instead of by marching along the trail. Artillery fire from Frederica forced the vessels to turn around. Oglethorpe pursued them with his scout boats.

A British seaman who had been captured by the Spaniards escaped and told Oglethorpe that Spanish morale was low. Oglethorpe planned a night raid to inflict more consternation on the invaders. On July 12 he led five hundred men, including the Highland Company, toward the fort occupied by the Spanish army. In the middle of the night, a French seaman with Oglethorpe's force fired his musket and alerted the Spaniards. The Frenchman fled into the woods, and later entered the Spanish camp. Oglethorpe's force returned to Frederica.

Oglethorpe sent a letter to the French seaman, knowing it would be intercepted by the Spanish commander. The letter made the French seaman seem to be in a conspiracy with Oglethorpe to deliver the Spaniards into an ambush. Once the letter was intercepted, the Spaniards lost trust in the French seaman's information.

When five ships from South Carolina appeared to the north of St. Simons Island, the Spanish forces sailed away before their avenue of escape could be cut off.

As the Spaniards moved southward toward Florida, they threatened the British garrison at Fort Prince William on Cumberland Island. Oglethorpe sent the garrison's commander a message ordering him to hold out until Oglethorpe could get there with reinforcements. The Spaniards thought the fort was defended by more men than the garrison actually contained, and called off their assault. Oglethorpe arrived two days later with a flotilla of scout boats. Oglethorpe's flotilla followed the Spanish fleet as far as northern Florida before returning to Frederica.

By August, Oglethorpe received support from ships of the Royal Navy and ships from South Carolina. Oglethorpe took the fleet to St. Augustine and attacked six Cuban half-galleys in the mouth of the harbor. A cannonball knocked the boom off the scout boat carrying Oglethorpe. A man in the boat was killed in the naval battle and two men were wounded. The battle ended at nightfall. Three days later, faced with strong winds and high surf, Oglethorpe's fleet left Florida.[46]

Oglethorpe returns to England

General James Edward Oglethorpe left Georgia forever on July 23, 1743, two years before the Jacobites would launch a final effort to restore the Stuarts to the throne of Great Britain. This coincidence of timing has inspired a bit of McIntosh family lore.

As preparations were underway for Oglethorpe's ship to set sail, so the story goes, William and Lachlan McIntosh were discovered hiding in the hold of another vessel. William and Lachlan were the teenage sons of John Mackintosh Mor, a nephew of Brigadier William Mackintosh of Borlum. The Brigadier had commanded a portion of the Jacobite forces attempting to restore the Stuarts to the throne of Great Britain in 1715. Now his great-nephews wanted to return to their birthplace in Scotland to assist in the next Jacobite rising. They wished not only to restore the Stuarts to the throne but also restore the Borlum branch of Clan Mackintosh to prominence. William McIntosh's grandson Thomas Spalding tells the story of what happened when Oglethorpe discovered that the boys were aboard:

> General Oglethorpe sent for the two young lads into his own cabin; he spoke to them of the friendship he entertained for their father, of the kindness he entertained for themselves, of the hopelessness of every attempt of the house of Stuart, of their own folly in engaging in this wild and desperate struggle, of his own duty as an officer of the house of Brunswick; but if they would go ashore, be hereafter quiet, and keep their own secret, he would forget all that had passed; – he received their pledge, and they never saw him again.[47]

John Mackintosh Mor returns to Georgia

Marjory Mackintosh and three of her children remained at Palachacola – where their relative John Mackintosh commanded the garrison – while her husband John Mackintosh Mor was a prisoner of war and their eldest sons William and Lachlan served in the regiment at Frederica. After nearly two years at Palachacola,

Marjory went back to Darien in anticipation that her husband would return. She retrieved her daughter Ann from the orphanage at Bethesda in September of 1742. John Mackintosh Mor was released from a Spanish jail in a prisoner exchange and arrived in Georgia late in 1743. Retaining his rank as captain, John Mackintosh Mor resumed command of the Highland Independent Company of Foot at Darien. When John Mackintosh Mor reunited with his wife and children, his son Lachlan left Frederica to live in the family home.[48]

The Jacobite Rising of 1745

During the Jacobite Rising of 1745, Aeneas the 22nd Chief of Clan Mackintosh serves in the government army while his wife Anne rallies the clan for the rebels. Clan Mackintosh suffers horrible casualties in the Battle of Culloden.

Mackintosh is dead; long live Mackintosh

The official Clan Mackintosh historian tells of the death of William the 21st Chief of Clan Mackintosh following the death of his wife Christian Menzies of Castle Menzies:

Christian died before her husband, who was much upset by her death.

William was a delicate man, who to improve his health went to the South of France, but returned to Edinburgh, where he died in 1740. He was buried at Holyrood, his funeral expenses were very moderate and none of the usual extravagance was allowed.[1]

Since William and his wife did not have children, his younger brother was next in line to the chieftainship.

Georgia historian Edward Cashin discusses the new leader of Clan Chattan, a confederation of clans led by the Chief of Clan Mackintosh:

The most important member of Clan Chattan to leave Georgia in 1740 was Captain Aeneas Mackintosh, commander at Fort

Palachacola. His reasons had nothing to do with the dissolution of the Darien community. His brother William, chief of the Clan of the Cat, died on September 24, 1740, and Aeneas succeeded to the title of Mackintosh of Mackintosh.

Captain Aeneas had served James Oglethorpe faithfully and well, and Oglethorpe wrote a generous recommendation to Duncan Forbes, lord president of the Court of Sessions at Inverness. "His long absence from his Country is the only reason that makes it necessary for me to recommend him, for otherwise his birth, being the Laird of Mackintosh's Brother, is such as would have made recommendation entirely needless."[2]

The ranger captain known as Aeneas Mackintosh on the Colonial American southern frontier was sometimes called by his Gaelic name Angus in Scotland. He succeeded as the 22nd Chief of Clan Mackintosh.[3]

The Chief of Mackintosh marries

Aeneas the 22nd Chief of Clan Mackintosh and Clan Chattan married Anne Farquharson, the eldest daughter of John Farquharson of Invercauld, the chief of that branch of Clan Chattan; her father had fought under the command of Brigadier William Mackintosh of Borlum in the Rising of 1715 and had been taken prisoner with the other Clan Chattan soldiers at Preston.

Men described Anne as both beautiful and accomplished, "a somewhat delicate-looking girl, with a retiring, modest look, elegant figure, and rather high forehead."[4]

A clan historian describes the marriage:

In 1741, at the age of 18, Anne married Aeneas Mackintosh of Mackintosh. The marriage contract, dated at Aberdeen 2 February 1741, was witnessed by her brother, several Farquharsons and Alexander MacGillivray of Dunmaglass. Aeneas had succeeded as 22nd Chief of his Clan only a few months earlier. He was considerably older than his bride, as much as 20 years perhaps, but from all accounts it was a happy and contented union. As Charles Fraser-Mackintosh was to observe, her letters show that "she threw herself... heart and soul into everything tending to the honour and prosperity of Mackintosh, and the haill Clan Chattan."

The newly-weds set up home in Moy Hall, built about 1700...[5]

The Rising of 1745

Charles Edward Stuart, who became known as Bonnie Prince Charlie, sought to restore his family to its rightful place in the world. His father claimed the titles King James III of England and James VIII of Scotland although he was in exile in Europe, and Charles was next in the line of succession of the historic dynasty. Their allies were called "Jacobites" from the Latin word for "James."

Clan historian Margaret Mackintosh of Mackintosh tells how Charles set off on his grand adventure:

News of the discontent in Scotland was carried to Rome where the so-called James VIII and his son, Prince Charles Edward, were living. It is important to know that the enthusiasm for the Stuarts or for actual rebellion in the Highlands was, over a long period, grossly exaggerated to the Old Pretender, the

Prince, and the French by the various Jacobite emissaries with subsequent fatal results. However, the Prince declared his intention of overthrowing King George II and of placing his father on the throne, and moved to France with great secrecy in January 1744. Delayed and disappointed by lack of support from King Louis XV, the Prince eventually set out for Scotland in a French ship, landing in the Western Highlands in July 1745.[6]

Prince Charles arrived in Scotland with only seven followers and plans to raise an army of Highlanders. Prince Charles led his army of Highlanders toward Edinburgh, the capital city of Scotland.

A French officer serving with the Jacobites described the scene when Charles proclaimed that his father James Stuart was the rightful king of Scotland and England:

...the Prince was conducted to Holyrood House, the palace of his ancestors, at the end of the suburbs, amidst the acclamations of an immense crowd, whom curiosity had brought to meet him a quarter of a league from the city. It was a new sight, Scotland having been deprived of the presence of its kings since the Revolution; and indeed they had seldom visited it since the union of the two crowns under James the First, son of the unfortunate Mary Stuart. The next day king James was proclaimed at Edinburgh, and the Prince named Regent to govern the kingdom, in the absence of his father, at Rome.[7]

Led by Ewan, younger of Cluny, the Macphersons – part of the confederation called Clan Chattan – joined the Jacobite army at Edinburgh.[8]

The Battle of Prestonpans: September 21, 1745

Sir John Cope, the government commander in Scotland, transported an army by ship from Aberdeen to the coast near Edinburgh. The army totaled 2,300 men and included cavalry and artillery.

The Highlanders who marched out to meet General Cope's army were about equal in number but were less well-armed. Some of them had various sorts of firearms such as muskets and fowling pieces but did not have swords, others had both firearms and broadswords, others had only swords, and about fifty of them had only a scythe blade attached to a pitchfork handle.[9]

General Cope established a strong strategic position near Prestonpans with defensive features including the sea, a marsh, and a boundary wall around the Preston House park. Military historian William Seymour describes the maneuver that penetrated the defenses:

> The Jacobite army, having passed... round the front of the enemy, still had to cross the marsh before reaching suitable ground over which to attack.
>
> One of their number, a local man called Robert Anderson, volunteered to show them a track that he knew well from snipe-shooting, and in the early hours of the morning he led the way. The mist swirled up from the bog as the wraith-like army wound its silent way through a defile near Riggonhead Farm and on through the morass. ...as day was breaking An-

derson had the army safely across the bank that divided the marsh from an open stubble field.

...The royalist infantry now had the unenviable task of facing the full fury of a Highland charge. ...as was their wont, having discharged a volley the Highlanders threw away their muskets and relied upon their broadswords, which, wielded with accuracy and vigour, bit deeply into the heads and limbs of the badly shaken redcoats.

General Cope and Lords Loudoun, Drummore and Home did their best to rally the terrified royalists... But all was chaos and confusion, and in a white heat of undisciplined passion the Highlanders laid about them, scattering the English army, until eventually the few officers and men who had tried to stem the flood joined the broad stream of fleeing men.[10]

Six Jacobite officers and about forty fighting men died in the battle. The Highlanders killed about three hundred English soldiers, took more than a thousand prisoners, and captured all the English baggage.

Even the Highlanders who carried only homemade weapons "did great execution with their scythes," an officer observed. "They cut the legs of the horses in two; their riders through the middle of their bodies."[11]

General Cope fled to Berwick.

Invasion of England

In an echo of Brigadier William Mackintosh's invasion of England in the Rising of 1715, Charles Edward led the Jacobite army toward London. In early November, the Jacobite army of 1745 crossed the Esk—where the Brigadier had stood in the middle of the river and cursed deserters as "reskels of humanity."

William Augustus, the Duke of Cumberland—King George II's third son—took command of the Royal army to oppose the army of Prince Charles. If Cumberland's army triumphed, his father would remain on the throne of Great Britain. If the army of Prince Charles triumphed, the Prince's father would reclaim the throne of his ancestors as King James III of Great Britain.

Rumors reached the Jacobites that many residents evacuated London carrying only their most valuable possessions and that King George II had ordered his yachts readied to carry him away at a moment's notice.

"It was at this juncture that King George and his court were said to be as struck with panic as if the wild McGillivrays were in the Strand," writes Edward Cashin.[12]

A detachment of the Jacobite army feinted toward Wales, drawing Cumberland's army away from London. The two wings of the Jacobite army rejoined at Derby, 120 miles from London.

In Scotland, meanwhile, government forces regained control of Edinburgh and Inverness. Highland clans loyal to the government formed regiments and independent companies that launched attacks on clans loyal to Prince Charles. Under those circumstances, the clan leaders participating in the invasion of England defied the Prince's wish to proceed toward London and demanded that the Jacobite army return to Scotland. This reversal of fortune threw the Prince into low spirits and caused the troops to lose morale.

As the Jacobites retreated from England, the Duke of Cumberland gave a mission to James Oglethorpe, who had named Cumberland Island off the coast of Georgia in the duke's honor.

Oglethorpe leads troops against Jacobites

After returning to England from Georgia, Oglethorpe had married Elizabeth Wright in 1744 and had moved from his family home to her estate in Cranham. He raised a volunteer unit for local defense that was named General Oglethorpe's Royal Foxhunters.[13] During the Jacobite Rising of 1745, Oglethorpe found himself at war with relatives of the Highlanders he had recruited to settle Darien in Georgia. Oglethorpe intended to do battle with relatives of the Highlanders he had led into battle at Bloody Marsh. "It was an ironic destiny that linked Oglethorpe's career with the Highland Scots," observes Georgia historian Edward Cashin. "They had been his best allies in Georgia; now they were his enemies... Among the clans that marched to the bagpipes were the Mackintoshes and Clan Chattan. Oglethorpe's friend Aeneas Mackintosh, chief of the clan, was not with them because he was a captain in the first royal Highland regiment."[14]

Military historian Larry Ivers explains how Oglethorpe was called upon to resist the Rising of 1745:

> Oglethorpe was commissioned a major general in March 1745. During the fall of that year he was in northern England with a volunteer regiment of horsemen and a few Georgia rangers, the latter having been recruited for duty in Georgia but temporarily diverted to help fight the Scottish rebels.
>
> When the rebels began their retreat toward the Scottish border in early December 1745 Oglethorpe was ordered to lead his horsemen in an encircling movement to cut them off. He pushed his soldiers over one hundred miles of unimproved roads that were covered with ice and snow in less than three days. They apparently arrived in a position from where

they could block the rebels' escape; however, that night Oglethorpe withdrew to a distance of five miles and did not begin his movement toward the enemy until about eleven o'clock the following morning. By then Prince Charles and his rebels had escaped. Criticism of his failure to halt the enemy's retreat began almost immediately. He and his horsemen were not allowed to accompany the army as it pursued Prince Charles…

…Two accusations were being voiced. First, it was suggested that he had not possessed the necessary courage to meet the Scots in battle. Second, it was rumored that he was in sympathy with the Jacobites, some of whom had been his active correspondents. Adding to the suspicion was the fact that the Oglethorpe family had previously exhibited Jacobite leanings. But he certainly did not lack courage, and his principal biographer was convinced that he had no political affiliation with the Jacobites. Oglethorpe's reasons for not setting out in pursuit until eleven o'clock were that his soldiers were exhausted, they had to forage for food, and they were outnumbered four to one.[15]

Edward Cashin adds some details about the attempt to block the retreat of the Jacobite army:

Oglethorpe, at the head of a regiment that included a company of Georgia rangers and accompanied by the faithful George Dunbar, now his aide-de-camp, was ordered to intercept the invaders at a village called Shap. The light-footed Scots got away. When the Duke of Cumberland learned about it he called out to Oglethorpe, "General Oglethorpe, had you done what I ordered you to do, few of these People would have escaped."

Oglethorpe demanded and received a court-martial. The testimony of Dunbar and others revealed that Oglethorpe had not slept for five nights before he reached Shap, that he was so ill that night that his officers feared for his life, that the duke's orders reached him late, and that weapons had to be put in order as the result of rain and sleet the previous day. Besides, the Scots slipped out at 4:30 in the morning before any attack could have been launched. Oglethorpe was acquitted…

The exoneration and promotion did not improve Oglethorpe's status in the opinion of the Duke of Cumberland. As long as the duke lived, Oglethorpe would never again command British troops. When Oglethorpe offered to raise a regiment in America during the Seven Years' War, he was ignored by Cumberland.[16]

Two government armies, one under the Duke of Cumberland and another under General George Wade, continued to pursue the fleeing Jacobites. Wade tried to intercept the Jacobites at Wigan, but like Oglethorpe did not succeed. The Highland rear guard – including Cluny Macpherson's regiment and the MacDonells of Glengarry – fought off Cumberland's advance guard at Clifton.

A French officer serving with the Jacobites described the army's return to Scotland:

We left Carlisle on the 20th of December, at three o'clock in the morning, and arrived on the bank of the river Esk, which separates Scotland from England, about two o'clock in the afternoon. This river, which is usually shallow, had been swelled by an incessant rain of several days, to a depth of four feet. However, we were obliged to cross it immediately, lest a continuation of the rain, during the night, should render the passage altogether impracticable. Our position was become extremely critical. We had not only to encounter all the English troops, but likewise the Hessians and Swiss, with six thousand Dutch, of the garrisons of Dendermonde and Tournay, who had been landed in England.

Nothing could be better arranged than the passage of the river. Our cavalry formed in the river to break the force of the current, about twenty-five paces above that part of the ford where our infantry were to pass; and the Highlanders formed themselves into ranks of ten or twelve a-breast, with their arms locked in such a manner as to support one another against the rapidity of the river, leaving sufficient intervals, between their ranks, for the passage of the water. Cavalry were likewise stationed in the river below the ford, to pick up and save those who might be carried away by the violence of the current. The interval between the cavalry appeared like a paved street through the river, the heads of the Highlanders being generally all that was seen above the water. By means of this contrivance, our army passed the Esk in an hour's time, without losing a single man; and a few girls, determined to share the fortune of their lovers, were the only persons who were carried away by the rapidity of the stream. Fires were kindled to dry our people as soon as they quitted the water; and the bagpipers having commenced playing, the Highlanders began all to dance, expressing the utmost joy on seeing their country again; and forgetting the chagrin which had incessantly devoured them, and which they had continually nourished ever since their departure from Derby.

We entered England on the 8th day of November, and left it on the 20th of December, the birth-day of the Prince, without losing more than forty men, either from sickness or marauding, including the twelve at the affair of Clifton-hall.

...As there is no town nearer than eight or ten miles from the ford of the Esk, we were obliged to march all night, though it had never ceased raining since the affair at Clifton-hall. Highlanders alone could have stood a march of two nights of continual rain in the midst of winter, and drenched as they were in crossing the river, but they were inured to fatigue, and of a strong and vigorous constitution, frequently marching six or seven leagues a-day, our ordinary marches in England, without leaving any stragglers behind...[17]

The Duke of Cumberland returned to London at the end of December, assigning General Henry Hawley the task of pursuing the Jacobites into Scotland. Hawley and Wade joined forces at Edinburgh.[18]

The Jacobite army, swelling to nine thousand men upon its return to Scotland, laid siege to the government garrison at Stirling Castle in January of 1746.

General Hawley set out from Edinburgh to relieve Stirling. Jacobite General Lord George Murray left a thousand men at Stirling and led most of the Jacobite army to oppose Hawley's advance. The government army and the Jacobite army were destined to do battle at Falkirk.[19]

Conflicting loyalties divide Clan Mackintosh

The horns of a dilemma gored Aeneas the 22nd Chief of Clan Mackintosh during the Rising of 1745. Both his clan and his wife's family had a heritage of loyalty to the Stuarts, while he also felt the pull of duty as an officer in the British army. Aeneas had commanded a fort on the colonial American southern frontier and he received another commission when he returned to Scotland. As a witness to treaties with the Creek Indians, he would have observed their strategy of exploiting the rivalry among the colonial powers. Highland clans adopted a similar strategy during the Jacobite Risings. "A favorite tactic was for the clan chiefs to remain at home, officially loyal to the government, while a son brought out the clan for the Stuarts," writes Frank McLynn, PhD. "Another was for a family to send one son to fight with the Hanoverians and another with the Jacobites." Referring to Aeneas Mackintosh by his Gaelic name, McLynn reports "In 1745 Angus, chief of the Mackintoshes, was on the Whig side, in the service of Lord Loudoun, but in his absence his young wife, Anne, raised the clan for Charles Edward."[20] McLynn continues, "As soon as her husband, a Hanoverian loyalist, departed to raise a company of militia for King George, 'Colonel Anne' raised the Mackintoshes for the prince. She then rode at their head in her tartan riding habit, with a clansman's blue bonnet on her head."[21]

Bruce Lenman, a professor of modern history at the University of St. Andrews, describes the situation:

> ...the Mackintoshes made a shamblingly indecisive entry onto the stage of the '45. Aeneas Mackintosh of Mackintosh held a captain's commission from George II... and he was married to a Jacobite spitfire of a wife, Anne, daughter of John Farquhar-

son of Invercauld. Mackintosh during the early stages of the rising seemed on the surface to be pursuing an ambiguous course. However, it is clear in retrospect that his main aim was to hinder the raising of recruits for the Jacobite army by potential rivals for the leadership of the Clan Chattan [a confederation of clans led by the Chief of Clan Mackintosh] and that he was throughout hand-in-glove with Duncan Forbes of Culloden. When, under the influence of the Lord President and MacLeod of MacLeod, he finally made it clear that he would not raise his clan for Prince Charles, his formidable lady raised it herself, making free use of force on reluctant tenants and earning the immortal title of 'Colonel Anne.'[22]

Clan Mackintosh and Clan Chattan historian Margaret Mackintosh of Mackintosh places the dilemma facing the Laird and Lady of Mackintosh in the context of military events in the Rising of 1745:

> ... at Derby it was decided in a Council of War to return to Scotland, and the army sadly retraced its steps. A party of Clan Chattan supporters joined the Prince at Stirling on his return. Cluny Macpherson attempted to enlist other Mackintoshes in Badenoch. However, the Chief of Mackintosh did not join the Prince, but continued to hold his commission under King George II and to command a company of the Black Watch. The Chief's wife, Anne Farquharson of Invercauld, though only twenty years old, took up the Prince's cause, and raised the clan without any hindrance from her husband. In his absence she inspected the clan regiment before it left for Stirling, selecting MacGillivray of Dunmaglas as Colonel.[23]

When Cluny Macpherson attempted to enlist men of Clan Mackintosh in the Jacobite cause, the Chief of Clan Mackintosh insisted on the privileges of rank. The Chief wrote to Cluny:

> Dear Sir, – As I am determined to command my own people and to run the same fate with them, having yesterday received a letter from the Prince, and another from the Duke of Atholl, I hope, notwithstanding the order you got from the Prince, you will not offer to meddle with any of my men, as we are both designed on the same errand. I am resolved to maintain the rank due to my family, and if you think proper to accept the next rank to me you will be very welcome...[24]

Clan Chattan historian Robert McGillivray views the predicament of Aeneas and Anne Mackintosh sympathetically:

> During their first years together, Anne was amusing herself at Moy Hall...
>
> This idyllic period came to an end in July 1745, however, with the arrival in Scotland of Prince Charles Edward Stuart. The previous year Aeneas Mackintosh had raised a Company for the Black Watch and had been commissioned to command it by the Government. His position, like that of many of the Clan chiefs, was a difficult one. He decided to stand aloof from the Jacobites, causing historians to speculate as to his motives.
>
> [In the words of their nephew Sir Aeneas Mackintosh]: "Pitying the prince for his misfortunes which he had not brought upon himself, she resolved to exert all her influence in

his behalf. She therefore took steps, soon after the commencement of the Rising, for embodying her husband's clan."

Calling on her close friend Alexander MacGillivray of Dunmaglass, she quickly formed a strong well-armed battalion which she placed under Dunmaglass' command. Perhaps because of this action in choosing a leader from outwith her immediate clan, or perhaps because they chose to follow the example of their Chief, the leading men of Clan Mackintosh were absent. Nonetheless it was a fine force, perhaps 800 strong, and Lady Mackintosh had earned her soubriquet "Colonel Anne."

Subsequent accounts described her in wildly romantic terms as riding at the head of her men, dressed in semi-masculine attire, pistols at her saddle-bow. Sir Walter Scott named her "a gallant Amazon."

...While General Stewart, an obvious admirer, observed "Of all the ladies who testified their Jacobite tendencies, few were more accomplished, more beautiful, or more enthusiastic than the Lady Mackintosh."

But it had taken time to make her decision and to raise the Clan. It was December before the Mackintosh Regiment was despatched south to join the Prince on his return from the venture into England. It was ready to take its place in the centre of the front line at the Battle of Falkirk on 17 January 1746, fighting with distinction alongside the Clan Macpherson Regiment and next but one to the Farquharsons under James of Balmoral.

Colonel Anne's father, having given his pledge to the Government and finding himself unable to persuade his own clansmen to refrain from rising, had left the Highlands and taken up residence in Leith.[25]

The Battle of Falkirk: January 17, 1746

Jacobite forces laid siege to Stirling Castle for two weeks before General Henry Hawley approached in an attempt to relieve the government garrison. Military historian David Smurthwaite tells what happened when the opposing armies came to grips:

Hawley's force of 8000 men advanced toward Stirling on 13 January 1746 and Charles, leaving 1000 Highlanders to screen the Castle, concentrated his army on Plean Muir. For the Jacobites the key position was a ridge of moorland rising steeply to the south-west of Falkirk about a mile from Hawley's camp. The forward slope of this ridge would provide an ideal springboard for a Highland charge, and on 17 January [Jacobite General Lord George] Murray advanced to occupy the ridge south-westwards and crossed the River Carron at Dunipace. Meanwhile a deception force under [Lord John] Drummond marched toward Falkirk on the main road from Bannockburn.

As Murray's Highlanders wound their way up the ridge from the west, Hawley at last realised the seriousness of his position and dispatched his three regiments of dragoons... up the eastern face. Both armies reached the crest in the midst of a rain storm and immediately deployed for battle. The Jacobites formed two lines with the first company, from left to right, the Appin Stewarts, Camerons, Frasers, MacPhersons, Mackintoshes, Farquharsons, and Macdonalds, and the second two battalions of the Atholl Brigade.

...Before his infantry had time to order its ranks, Hawley launched the dragoons... in a charge against the Jacobite right. A shattering volley of musketry delivered when the dragoons were within ten yards of the Highland line brought down eighty horsemen and most of the survivors turned and fled.

Careering from the field pursued by the Macdonalds, the dragoons crashed into the Hanoverian left wing and the Glasgow Volunteers, scattering men in every direction. Having already discharged their muskets and being unable to reload because of the lashing rain, the Highland centre drew swords and charged.

Equally hampered by damp powder, the Hanoverian centre fired a desultory volley at the approaching clansmen and then ran for their lives.

Only on the right, where the infantry were protected from a charge by the ravine, did any regiments hold their position. Here Ligionier's, Price's, and Barrel's Regiments joined forces and advanced up the hill to enfilade the advancing Highland line. So effective was this fire that the pursuit stopped and the Highland ranks began to waver, with many clansmen leaving the field convinced they had been defeated.

The situation was reversed by the arrival of the Irish picquets who obliged the three Hanoverian regiments to follow the rest of their army along the road to Linlithgow.

Night was falling and Murray, with his own regiments dispersed over the countryside, was content to occupy Falkirk and the enemy camp where quantities of arms, provisions and wines quickly found new owners.

The Jacobite loss had been small with not more than 50 dead and 80 wounded, but Hanoverian casualties were substantial with perhaps 350 dead and over 300 taken prisoner. The battle had lasted little more than twenty minutes.[26]

After the English army retreated to Edinburgh, the Jacobites resumed the siege of Stirling without success. At the beginning of February, the Jacobites abandoned the siege and moved into the Highlands to spend the winter.

Meanwhile, the Duke of Cumberland resumed his pursuit of his rival Prince Charles. Cumberland's army moved as far as Perth before being stopped by wintry weather.[27]

The Rout of Moy: February 16, 1746

As Prince Charles traveled from Stirling toward Inverness, he stopped along the way at Moy Hall, the seat of Clan Mackintosh. With the Chief of Clan Mackintosh away on service in the government army, Prince Charles could count on being hospitably received by Lady Anne Mackintosh, who had raised her clan in support of the Prince. She provided supper for ten people at the Prince's table, eight aide de camps at another table in the same room, and at least seventy servants in the Prince's household. The master of the Prince's household called the supper "exceedingly genteel and plentiful."[28]

Meanwhile, twelve miles away in Inverness, government officials learned that Prince Charles was at Moy. At evening, they sent out Lord Loudon with at least fifteen hundred troops on a mission to capture the Prince. Margaret Mackintosh of Mackintosh describes the result in *The History of the Clan Mackintosh and the Clan Chattan:*

... The Lady Mackintosh sent out Donald Fraser, the Smith at Moy, with four other men to watch the road from Inverness. About midnight, when they became aware of the approach of a body of troops, Fraser posted his men among a number of peat-stacks which might be mistaken in the darkness for groups of men. When Loudon's troops came near, Fraser and his men fired their guns and ran in various directions shouting loudly for the Mackintoshes, Camerons and Macdonalds to advance. The ruse was successful, and the army fell back in alarm to Inverness. At the same time a small boy was smuggled out of Inverness by old Lady Mackintosh, who was Anne Duff, widow of the twentieth Chief, to warn the Prince of Loudon's approach. The boy was secretly carried out on horseback under the cloak of a dragoon, and once outside the town he slipped off the horse to make his way by short-cuts to Moy. He gave the alarm, the Prince was aroused and left Moy Hall to join Lochiel's men, who were preparing to make a stand, when a messenger came to tell them of the Smith's success, which came to be known as the Rout of Moy. The Smith's sword and anvil are still kept at Moy Hall, and so are Prince Charles' bonnet and the bed he slept in.

Lord Loudon, thinking the Jacobite army much larger than it actually was, withdrew his troops immediately from Inverness. Accordingly, Prince Charles took possession of the town as his headquarters, staying for two months in the house of the dowager Lady Mackintosh, in Church Street.[29]

Robert McGillivray, who calls the Rout of Moy "part of Clan lore," describes the commotion when the Prince learned of the approaching enemy:

...In the small hours of the morning of Monday 17th February, the whole household at Moy Hall was awakened; the Prince by one of his guards. James Gib [who served as "Master-Household in the Prince's service] observed the scene: "and in the close he saw the Prince walking with his bonnet above his nightcap, and his shoes down in the heels; and Lady Mackintosh in her smock petticoat running through the close, speaking loudly and expressing her anxiety about the Prince's safety." Lady Mackintosh and her sister issued hurried orders to the servants as they sought to make provision to safeguard the Prince. He was escorted by thirty Highlanders down to the side of Loch Moy for about a mile where they joined up with the Camerons, ready to make a stand if necessary. James Gib said he "went along with the Prince down the side of the loch, and left several covered wagons and other baggage at Moy, about which Lady Mackintosh forbad Mr. Gib to be in the least anxious, for that she would do her best to take care of them. And indeed she was as good as her word: for upon the Prince's return to Moy, Mr. Gib found all his things in great safety, the most of them having been carried off by Lady Mackintosh's orders into a wood, where they would not readily have been discovered, though Lord Loudon and his men had proceeded to Moy."

Alexander Stewart, who was in the kitchen that evening, described what was happening in Moy Hall itself. "My Lady McIntosh and her sister and me went to the rooms where he sleept and took all the most valuable things that were in the roome where he lay and went upe to the garrats and hide them in fether stands that was almost full of feathers, and my

Lady was always calling at me to follow with the curtains for I would stay till they would take me by the neck, for by this time the Prince was more than a mile towards the southwest of the loch thorrou a wood."

Welcome news of the rout of the Government troops in the pass was enough to send a messenger after the Prince, advising him to return to Moy Hall. He was glad to do so. He was suffering from exposure to the early morning frost and contacted a very bad cold from which he was to suffer for some time. Nonetheless he spent the rest of that day gathering his army together and the following morning advanced and occupied the town of Inverness from which the Hanoverians had fled.[30]

Being part of clan lore, the tale of the Rout of Moy has been told many times, many ways. In an article in *The Celtic Monthly* published in 1902, Angus MacKintosh tells the tale in a dramatic style:

[Lady Mackintosh] sent Donald Fraser, a doughty blacksmith, and five other men on whom she could rely to watch the road between Inverness and Moy. There were Hanoverian troops in Inverness, and also clans who supported the Hanoverian Government. Lord Loudon was there with 1700 men, eager to distinguish himself, and he was kept well informed of the Prince's movements by the Grants of Strathspey and others. On the very day on which the Prince arrived at Moy, Loudon heard that he was there, and promptly made arrangements for a surprise.

Having placed sentinels round the town to prevent any Jacobites from giving the alarm, he waited until nightfall, and then went forth with 1500 men. The night was dark, with frequent flashes of lightning. MacLeod of MacLeod was amongst those in front, with his trusty piper MacCrimmon (who played when they were leaving Dunvegan the prophetic Lament that shall ever be associated with his name "Cha till mi tullidh") by his side.

When they reached Faillie Bridge, the blacksmith and his men who were watching, fell back unobserved, and stationed themselves among some peat stacks beside the road near the Pass of Crag-nan-eoin. Silently the 1500 marched on, never doubting but success would crown their lordly leader's plan, until out of the darkness flashed tongues of flame, and a few of them fell, amongst whom was MacCrimmon. Then the war-cries of Lochiel, MacKintosh, Keppoch, and other Jacobite clans rang in their ears. Thinking that the Prince's whole army was in front of them they wheeled round and in great confusion fled. Their opponents, however, were only the blacksmith and his little band, who, when they had fired their muskets, separated and ran hither and thither shouting the war-cries of the clans, and giving orders as if they were leading men to battle.

Meanwhile a messenger from Inverness reached Moy with the intelligence that Loudon was on his way to take the Prince by surprise. Accounts differ as to who the messenger was. Once is that the Dowager Lady MacKintosh, who resided in Inverness at the time, sent a youth named Lachlan MacKintosh, who knew the short byways from Inverness to Moy, with the message; another is that the bearer of the alarm was a young girl from Moy, serving in a tavern in Inverness, who overheard some of Loudon's officers talking about the intended surprise over their cups, who succeeded in eluding the sentinels and with all speed made her way to Moy: and that when she told Lady MacKintosh her story she fell down dead from over-exertion. The incident, according to the latter version, has been put into excellent verse by Miss Alice MacDonell, the gifted bardess of Keppoch. The commotion into which Moy was thrown by this intelligence did not last long, for the blacksmith arrived shortly after with an account of the rout.

On the 18th February the Prince, whose men had then arrived at Moy, marched to Inverness, but only to find that Loudon had retired into Ross-shire.[31]

Sir Fitzroy Maclean of Dunconnel, author of the splendidly illustrated *Highlanders: A History of the Scottish Clans*, elaborates on the fate of the ill-starred piper:

Almost the only casualty in the Rout of Moy, as it came to be called, was MacLeod of MacLeod's personal piper, Donald Ban MacCrimmon, of the famous family of pipers from Skye, whose Chief had sent him against his will to serve against Prince Charles and who, having the second sight and foreseeing his own death in a cause which he abhorred, composed for the occasion the haunting lament *Cha till, Cha till, Cha till MacCraimein,* MacCrimmon will not return.[32]

The tale about the girl who ran to warn the Prince may have originated in the memoirs of the Chevalier de Johnstone, translated from a French manuscript:

Whilst some English officers were drinking in the house of Mrs. Bailly, an innkeeper in Inverness, and passing the time till the hour of their departure, her daughter, a girl of thirteen or fourteen years of age, who happened to wait on them, paid great attention to their conversation, and, from certain expressions dropped by them, she discovered their designs. As soon as this generous girl was certain as to their intentions, she immediately left the house, escaped from the town, notwithstanding the vigilance of the centinels, and immediately took the road to Moy, running as fast as she was able, without shoes or stockings, which to accelerate her progress, she had taken off, in order to inform the Prince of the danger that menaced him.

She reached Moy, quite out of breath, before Lord Loudon; and the Prince, with difficulty, escaped in his robe de chamber, night-cap, and slippers, to the neighbouring mountains, where he passed the night in concealment.

This dear girl, to whom the Prince owed his life, was in great danger of losing her own, from her excessive fatigue on this occasion; but the care and attentions she experienced restored her to life, and her health was at length re-established.[33]

Mackintosh versus Mackintosh

Even after Lord Loudon's forces withdrew northward they continued to harass the Jacobite army under Prince Charles at Inverness. Meanwhile, the Duke of Cumberland had advanced to Aberdeen, so that the Jacobite army was threatened by government armies in two directions. Prince Charles sent a detachment to pursue Lord Loudon's Regiment of Foot, in which Aeneas the

22nd Chief of Clan Mackintosh served as a captain. The Jacobite detachment pursuing Lord Loudon included the Mackintosh regiment, according to the clan historian. Other clans participating in the expedition included Glengarry, Clanranald, Stewart of Appin, the Frasers, MacGregors, MacKinnons and MacKenzies.

Loudon retreated as far north as Sutherland, and eluded the pursuers by crossing and recrossing the Dornoch Firth. He had commandeered all the boats, and the Jacobites had to march around the firth. The Jacobites collected boats at Findhorn and took them northward past British warships in a heavy fog. On March 20, about a thousand Jacobites commanded by the Duke of Perth landed in Sutherland in pursuit of two thousand government troops. The Jacobites marched on Dornoch, where Loudon had set up headquarters.[34]

The stage was set for a civil war not only among the Mackintosh clan but also among other Highlanders who served in Loudon's Regiment and their fellow clansmen in the Jacobite army. Donald of Scotus, a MacDonell clansman, was usually cheerful but as his detachment prepared to attack Lord Loudon he had tears in his eyes. "A son whom I adore is an officer in his regiment," Donald told a friend. "I thought myself fortunate in being able to procure such a situation for his youth, being unable to anticipate the landing of the Prince in Scotland. Perhaps tomorrow I may be so unfortunate as to kill my son with my own hand; and thus the same ball which I fire in my defense may give to myself the most cruel death. However, in going with the detachment I may be able to save him; and if I do not go he may fall by the hands of another."[35]

The Jacobite forces captured Loudon's headquarters at Dornoch on March 30, taking three hundred prisoners. Lord Loudon withdrew to the Isle of Skye and the Jacobites returned to Inverness.[36]

Aeneas the 22nd Chief of Clan Mackintosh was among several Highlanders in Lord Loudon's regiment who avoided battle against their kinsmen by surrendering, according to Donald MacDonnell of Lochgarry:

> The laird of McIntosh, capt. in Loudon's regiment, and Major McKenzie of the same, with several other officers (including Ranald MacDonnell, son of Donald of Scotus whom his own father had the good fortune to take prisoner) came and surrendered themselves prisoners, with all the men under their command ... Capt. Stack of Laly's regiment and I received the arms of the whole prisoners.[37]

Aeneas Mackintosh's surrender give rise to a legendary belief that "Colonel Anne" Mackintosh led the soldiers who "captured the Hanoverian captain who happened to be her husband."[38] Ranald MacDonnell's surrender gave rise to a scene recorded in the memoirs of the Chevalier de Johnstone:

> ...I heard a loud knocking at my door; and running to it, I perceived this good father [Donald of Scotus], holding a handsome young man by the hand. He instantly called out, with eyes sparkling with joy, "Here, my friend, here is he, who caused me yesterday so much anxiety. I took him prisoner myself, and, having secured him, I troubled myself very little about taking others." He then shed tears of joy; very different from the tears of the preceding evening. We supped all three together in my apartment, and I scarcely ever enjoyed more

satisfaction than in witnessing this tender scene between the father and son.[39]

After Aeneas the 22nd Chief of Clan Mackintosh was taken prisoner, a Clan Chattan historian writes:

> The Prince released him into the care of his wife, saying he could not be more secure or more honourably treated. Chambers, incorrectly describes Anne as "then acting a semi-military part in the chevalier's army", and goes on to tell how when she encountered her husband: "She said, with military laconism: 'Your servant, Captain!' to which he replied, with equal brevity, 'Your servant, Colonel!'" A nice little anecdote, whether true or not.[40]

Another keeper of clan lore, Angus MacKintosh, states that Aeneas Mackintosh was held prisoner in Inverness although "the Prince is said to have jocularly remarked that he had better make MacKintosh's wife his custodian."[41]

The Battle of Culloden: April 16, 1746

At Aberdeen, the Duke of Cumberland spent February and March drilling his troops in tactics designed to counter the Highland charge. The infantrymen were trained to engage the enemy soldier to their right rather than the enemy directly ahead. The Highlanders, with their sword in one hand and their shield, called a target, in the other hand could not defend themselves against a bayonet attack from the side.[42]

In April, when the roads were free of snow and the River Spey was low enough to ford, Cumberland moved toward Inverness.

Prince Charles led his army out of Inverness to make a stand near Culloden House. When Cumberland reached Nairn, the Jacobites decided to launch a surprise attack. After the Highlanders marched all night to reach Nairn, the attack was called off and they marched back to Culloden. Because their supplies had been left in Inverness, they had nothing to eat. Starved of both sleep and food, some of them lay down on the ground and some went foraging. When Jacobite officers told Prince Charles that the men were not fit for battle, he observed that they were too fatigued to conduct an orderly retreat.

Cumberland's troops, meanwhile, had slept through the night. Early in the morning, they ate breakfast, sipped brandy, and marched toward Culloden. Heavy showers were falling when the opposing armies – about eight thousand government troops against about five thousand Jacobites – came within sight of one another across two miles of open moor. For the first time in the Rising, the armies exchanged artillery fire. The Jacobite artillery nearly knocked the Duke of Cumberland off his big gray horse, while the government artillery aimed at Prince Charles, killing his groom and some cavalrymen. Many of the Jacobite artillerymen fled when the government artillery opened fire, and within a few minutes all but one of the Jacobite guns had ceased firing. The English guns, however, roared on. Gunpowder blew in the faces of the Highlanders as shot plowed through their ranks. Without an order to launch their famous Highland Charge, the clansmen huddled in ranks and endured the English cannonade for nearly half an hour. Hundreds of them fell dead or wounded, others lay on the ground to avoid the artillery shells, and some ran away seeking safety.[43]

Military historian Peter Harrington describes the battle in *Culloden 1746: The Highland Clans' Last Charge*:

Shortly before 1:30 p.m., with a squall of hail and rain lashing the clansmen, the order to charge was given. Lord George Murray, who described the regiments in the front rank as 'so impatient that they were like to break their ranks', had been approached by several clan leaders anxious for a decision and fearful that they would be unable to hold their men much longer amidst the terrible slaughter. The restive Mackintoshes urged their leader, Lochiel, to persuade Murray to order the charge. Murray sent Kerr of Graden to the Prince who consented to the attack. By now the Jacobite line was skewed, the right wing being well in advance of the left, so Kerr directed the Duke of Perth on the left to move to the attack. Laclan MacLachan, one of Charles's aides-de-camp, was sent to Murray, who was with the Athollmen on the right, to order the attack, but was killed by round shot before he got to the front. Further delay ensued, while more and more casualties were sustained. Charles then sent Sir John Macdonald to the left and Brigadier Stapleton to the right with orders for the line to advance. The order was received, but the Macdonalds refused and were urged on only a few paces level with the other regiments in the front line.

In rage and despair the Mackintoshes of the Clan Chattan in the centre 'scrugged' their bonnets over their heads, broke the ragged line and darted forward through the wet heather, spurred-on by the pipes and by their commander, the yellow-haired Colonel MacGillivray. Grape-shot continued to pepper the oncoming clansmen. At their heels came the men of Atholl and the Camerons who had been positioned on the right of the Clan Chattan, but the direction of their charge changed suddenly towards the left to avoid some walls and toward the firmer ground of an old moor road. At the same time, the Mackintoshes veered right to avoid the boggy ground between the two armies, and possibly forced by the heavy musketry which opened up from the centre of the Royal ranks. Confused and blinded by smoke, many were lost in the mêlée, or fell to the brisk firing from the Royal centre. Survivors later stated that they were caught in thick smoke and became disoriented. The Clan Chattan lost eighteen officers and hundreds of men before getting within twenty yards of the Royal lines. Similarly, the Athollmen were cut down before they had a chance to engage. They had run broadsides to Wolfe's men lining the wall who decimated them with accurate musket fire. The walls on each flank had a funneling effect, forcing the charging clansmen into an area little more than 300 yards wide. Undeterred, the dense mass now crammed into this narrow corridor against the park wall and the Leanach dike, and moved towards the left of the Duke's army to engage the men of Barrell's, Munro's and Wolfe's Regiments. In the few seconds it took to cover the distance, many of the Highlanders, unable to fire their customary volley because of the congestion, discarded their primed muskets and pistols and resorted to the broadsword, scythe blades or axes. For a moment the Prince's soldiers were shrouded in cannon smoke, but as it lifted they saw an orderly line of Redcoats, 30 yards away, who leveled their muskets and fired an accurate and deadly volley; a distinctive counterpoint to the monotonous pounding of [English artillery commander Brevet-Colonel William] Belford's guns which continued to fire. The troops in the front ranks knelt to fire while two other ranks stood behind with muskets raised to shoulder, providing continuous firing as one line after another reloaded. The enfilade fire from Wolfe's men in front of the Leanach dike was now beginning to take effect, but the shouting Highlanders came on pell-mell towards the left.

...Towards the centre and left, the Highlanders were faring little better. The advance of the Clan Chattan and others on the right had inspired others to follow. The MacLeans and MacLachlans charged, but – the rebel lines being skewed – they had further open ground to cover and none reached the Royal lines; the musket fire from the Royals and Pulteney's was so deadly that no living thing could survive. Of the 200 MacLeans, whose boast it was that they never gave ground, 150 were killed. Keppoch and Macdonnell of Scothouse [Donald of Scotus] died in the thick of the action, the latter only twenty paces from the enemy. The dead ground between the two armies was littered with dead and dying clansmen. Less enthusiastic were the Farquharsons and the Macdonalds. Since early morning the Macdonalds of the Glengarry Regiment had been complaining about their placement on the extreme left of the Jacobite line, and the Duke of Perth had tried to placate them. When the Regiment saw the Highlanders' charge on the right and centre they advanced a few paces and began to run towards the Royal lines, firing pistols and waving their swords in the vain hope of tempting the Royal troops to attack. Some fell into knee-deep water and could advance no further because of the swampy ground. They were swept back by musket fire, it being said by Cumberland that his infantry 'hardly took their firelocks from their shoulders' and, seeing activity amongst the Royal cavalry suggesting a flanking movement, started to retrace their steps, just as other clans in the rear began to flee the field. Some officers charged with Keppoch, but many including the leader were felled by musket balls. A number of the Macdonalds were brought off by picquets before they could be surrounded by Kingston's Horse. The guns of the Royal artillery continued to fire relentlessly and stragglers were still being killed by grape-shot. To add to the slaughter Cobham's 60 troopers and Kingston's Horse moved off from the Royal lines and rode in amongst the fugitives, hacking at them without mercy. The Jacobite lines were in complete disarray, with gaps left by the fleeing clansmen. The battle had been raging for less than half-an-hour, but the left and centre of the army no longer existed.[44]

Realizing that the cause was lost, Prince Charles was escorted from the field by remnants of two Highland regiments. The English artillery ceased firing for the first time in an hour. Government troops crossed the field and bayoneted wounded Jacobites. Saber-wielding cavalrymen pursued fleeing Highlanders, hacking to death any clansmen who stood their ground. The cavalrymen also killed noncombatants, including two men plowing a field. Some of the fleeing Highlanders were killed by fellow Highlanders, Campbell clansmen of the Argyll Militia in the government army.

The government reported casualties of fifty killed and 259 wounded. An estimated two thousand clansmen died—including Alexander MacGillivray of Dunmaglass, the commander of the Mackintosh regiment—and 558 Jacobites were taken prisoner.[45]

Margaret Mackintosh of Mackintosh describes the battle from the perspective of her clan:

> The Jacobite leaders, thinking that the Duke of Cumberland would celebrate his birthday, decided on a night attack while the Duke's men would be sleeping off the effects of the festivity. The Jacobites had about ten miles to travel, and as they started at eight o'clock in the evening they should have been there by midnight. However, they had not come up with the enemy by two o'clock in the morning, and all hope of a surprise attack was abandoned. The weary and half-famished Highlanders were led back to the fatal moor of Culloden, which they reached about five o'clock in the morning. News came that the enemy was advancing, and the Jacobite army was at once drawn up in battle array. They were nearly starving, and the only food they obtained was one biscuit per man. Some others had gone into Inverness to find food for themselves. The enemy consisted of eight thousand fresh, well-fed troops, supported by plenty of cavalry and cannon.
>
> The battle began at one o'clock on the 16th April. The Camerons were placed on the right, with the Mackintoshes in the centre and the Macdonalds on the left. Charles had unfortunately selected for their battlefield the open moor where Cumberland's horse could make good use of the ground. Another blunder was that Charles kept his little force waiting to be attacked. For some time they stood firm and were raked by a terrible cannon fire, while to add to their misery a snowstorm beat mercilessly on their faces. The Mackintosh regiment, unable to refrain, broke from the front line and charged, to be followed by the rest of the line.

What followed was a foregone conclusion. The Highlanders rushed ahead in a last despairing charge; regardless of their hunger, regardless of their frozen limbs, driven to a frenzy by their misery and inspired by their hatred of their English foes, the little band swept forward to its doom. Not once did it falter though three lines of steady muskets, and cannon loaded with grape-shot made cruel gaps in its ranks. Forward it rushed. It reached its goal, broke through the first line of English, whom it swept aside like chaff; almost reached the second line, and then it melted, literally mown down. All that loyalty, all that heroism could do was done that day, and done in vain. Unsupported by the rest of the army the first forlorn hope could do no more. The Mackintosh regiment which led the fatal charge suffered the most severely, and more Mackintoshes were killed than any other clan. Out of seventeen officers only eight were surviving. The day after the battle the Highlanders were found lying in heaps three to four deep, so eager were those behind to reach their foes. …so numerous were the Mackintosh casualties that their massed graves are commemorated by three grave-stones.[46]

Angus MacKintosh hints at legends arising from "feats of prowess and valour" performed by his clansmen during the battle:

But the dark day of Culloden with its sad tale of mismanagement, hunger, jealousy, pride and disaster drew near. In the futile night march to Nairn the MacKintoshes were in the front and on the moor the next day they were the first to close with the foe. Galled with the enemy's fire they rushed forward before the order was given, and bravely they acquitted themselves. Out of 22 officers and 700 men, they left 19 officers and 400 men dead on the field. To tell of the feats of prowess and valour performed by many of them in that wild charge – from Gillies MacBean defending the breach in the wall, to Donald MacKintosh saving the banner, when all else was lost – would take too much space.[47]

Military historians Brigadier Peter Young and Professor John Adair describe horrid hand-to-hand combat:

…Barrel's regiment was borne backwards by the sheer weight of the mass of charging men. Captain Lord Robert Kerr received a Cameron on his spontoon, as his men gave way, and was cut down by Major Gillies MacBean of the Mackintosh regiment, his head 'cleft from crown to collar-bone'.

Lt.-Colonel Robert Rich of Barrel's was terribly wounded, six cuts in the head, his left hand lopped off, and his right arm nearly severed above the elbow. Ensign Brown was wounded defending a colour. But Barrel's fought back like heroes; Michael Hughes, a volunteer in Bligh's regiment, could see the officers, 'some cutting with their swords, others pushing with their spontoons, the sergeants running their halberts into the throats of the enemy, while the soldiers mutually defended each other… ramming their bayonets up to the socket.'[48]

The Dowager Lady Mackintosh jailed

Cumberland's army occupied Inverness in the afternoon after the Battle of Culloden. The victors, after releasing Argyll militiamen and other loyalist captives from prison in Inverness, promptly placed captured Jacobite soldiers in the prison. In what must have been more than coincidence, the Duke of Cumberland—the third son of King George II—set up headquarters at Inverness in the same house that Charles—the son of the would-be King James III—had used as his quarters. Margaret Mackintosh of Mackintosh writes:

> ...Cumberland pursued his victorious march to Inverness, which he entered without opposition. There he stayed in the house of the Dowager Lady Mackintosh, in the very room and the same bed which Prince Charles had so lately occupied. The old lady, speaking afterwards of those events, was wont to remark: 'I've had two King's bairns living with me in my time, and to tell you the truth I wish I may never have another.'
>
> She was confined for fourteen days in the common guard as were also several other ladies attached to the Jacobite cause.[49]

Lady Anne Mackintosh imprisoned

The victorious government forces soon began systematically persecuting the Jacobite clans. It wasn't long before government troops made the short trip from Inverness to the Mackintosh clan seat at Moy. Angus MacKintosh describes the scene:

> ...On the 17th of April a detachment of Col. Cockayne's regiment was sent to Moy to bring in all the cattle they could find there, and another detachment of the same regiment was sent the same day to take Lady MacKintosh to Inverness. Some of the men, who seem to have reached Moy Hall in advance of the main body, behaved brutally. In her zeal for the Prince's

cause Lady MacKintosh sent every man about the place who could wield a sword to Culloden, and those who survived of them were scattered on the mountains. There only remained a few women and one or two infirm old men. The soldiers at first took her for a girl, and inquired for "the ------ rebel Lady MacKintosh."

Mr. Lesley, the minister of Moy, who saw the men approaching Moy Hall, hastened thither, thinking he would be able to prevent them from committing acts of rudeness, but they heeded him not. He took out his watch and one of the men snatched it from him. Seeing this Lady MacKintosh offered the man a guinea to return the watch. He took the coin and then snatched the purse, which contained fifty guineas, all the money she had, from her. Another soldier insisted that she had more money, and struck her with his bayonet. It was then that another of the soldiers recognised her as the young lady who in Perth years before saved him from a flogging. He immediately showed his gratitude by seizing her cowardly assailant, and threatening his life if he did not desist. On the main body coming up another recognition took place. Sir Everard Falconer, Cumberland's secretary, found the "Amazonian Colonel Anne" they were sent to make prisoner, was in reality the slim, beautiful, and accomplished Miss Farquharson whom he once knew and greatly admired, slim and beautiful as in her maiden days. He wanted to apprehend the brutal soldiers, but she begged him to do nothing further in the matter.

She was then mounted on the only horse left at Moy and taken to Inverness. Great was the curiosity of the English soldiers to see the lady of whom such extraordinary tales, which they believed, were told. When near Cumberland's camp, the old war-horse she rode pricked up his ears, and much against her will carried her to where the drummers were beating their drums. "O!" said they, "that is the horse on which she charged at the head of her men at Falkirk and Culloden."

She was kept in custody at Inverness for six weeks, and this is how the arch-coward Hawley expressed his wishes concerning her at the Duke of Cumberland's table: "D--- that rebel Lady Mackintosh, I shall honour her with a mahogany gallows and a silken cord," language well befitting the craven of Falkirk, and not out of place at the table of the Butcher.[50]

Another clan historian, Robert McGillivray, picks up the thread of the tale:

Colonel Anne was placed in custody by order of the Duke of Cumberland and kept under guard in her own room. She seems to have been reasonably well treated herself, but was extremely concerned for the well-being of fellow prisoners, who were kept in appalling conditions. While there she heard that enemies of her husband, also on the Government side, had gone to Moy. She was able to alert him to the danger and he arrived with his men in time to protect the house.[51]

Margaret Mackintosh of Mackintosh continues the narrative:

In consequence of a Government order to deprive the Jacobites of their arms, a party was sent to Strathdearn to seize all the weapons. Grant of Dalrachny went to Moy and took the famous swords, which were heirlooms, to wit, the swords of

Charles I and of Dundee, and two dating from the battle of the North Inch, 1396. Mackintosh [the 22nd Chief of Clan Mackintosh] at once got Lord Loudon to ask the Duke to have them restored. This was granted, but Mackintosh got word that his family papers were being destroyed. He hastened to Moy, where he found the Grants had seized many Charters and documents which he had placed for safety in the Castle on the island. The Grants were already burning the precious papers, but Mackintosh had a force of two hundred men and dispersed the evil-doers and saved most of his valuable records.[52]

After six weeks of imprisonment, Lady Mackintosh was released into the custody of her husband.[53]

Prince Charles eludes pursuit

"The months," writes Theo Aronson in *Kings over the Water: The Saga of the Stuart Pretenders*, "that Prince Charles spent in Scotland as a hunted fugitive are generally regarded as the most praiseworthy of his life. This has become his finest hour. Sometimes alone, sometimes with a handful of companions, he survived a series of extraordinary adventures. He endured hardships, ran incredible risks, affected disguises, achieved hair's-breadth escapes, commanded touching loyalty and revealed a daring and a vigour and an optimism that was to become legendary. Although he had a price of £30,000 on his head, he was never once betrayed. The story of that great adventure is as much a testimony to the loyalty of the Scottish people as to Charles's heroism."[54]

After dodging pursuers through the bens, glens and islands for six months, Charles boarded a French ship and escaped from Scotland.

Lady Anne dances with Duke of Cumberland

A few Highlanders remained loyal to the Stuart dream and were willing to suffer the consequences. Among them was Lady Anne Mackintosh, the wife of the 22nd Chief of Clan Mackintosh. She had been imprisoned for six weeks for her role as "Colonel Anne" in the Rising of 1745 but she never relinquished her combative spirit. In 1748, Lady Anne visited London and attended a ball given by William Augustus, the Duke of Cumberland, who had commanded the British forces that had quelled the Rising. He asked her to dance when the musicians played a song in his honor: "Up and waur them a' Willie." After dancing with him to his tune, she asked him to dance with her to her tune. He gallantly complied and she asked for the tune "The auld Stuarts back again."[55]

Mackintosh is dead; long live Mackintosh

The chieftainship of Clan Mackintosh went through a succession when Aeneas, 22nd Chief of Clan Mackintosh, died in 1770. His nephew Aeneas Mackintosh succeeded as the 23rd Chief of Clan Mackintosh

Lady Anne Mackintosh – the legendary "Colonel Anne" of the Rising of 1745 – moved to Edinburgh after the death of her husband the 22nd Chief. "There," clan historian Angus MacKintosh writes, "far from Moy, she doubtless often mused on the stirring days she had seen, and the brave clansmen that rose round her to fight and die for Bonnie Prince Charlie."[56]

The Last Laird of Borlum

Edward Mackintosh 7th of Borlum becomes known as the last laird of Borlum. The heir of the line of Borlum may be found in the descendants of John Mackintosh Mor.

Borlum is dead; long live Borlum

John Mackintosh Mor's cousin Shaw the 6th of Borlum died about 1770 and was succeeded by his only son Edward as 7th of Borlum. By that time the estate of Borlum had been sold to satisfy creditors, so Edward lived at Raits in Badenoch.

The last laird of Borlum

Edward 7th of Borlum became known as the last laird of Borlum. Clan historian William Fraser Ross acknowledges that Edward was a controversial figure. "Tales of his wrongdoing are legion, many of them, no doubt, pure fiction," Ross writes. "It is a fact, however, that in 1773, Edward had to flee the country for an armed attack on a Ross-shire drover of the name of McRory, but his illegitimate brother, Alexander, was apprehended, tried, found guilty and suffered the extreme penalty of the law in 1773. It is believed that Edward made his way to America, and that he made some atonement for his past crimes in the ranks of the Army of his adopted country."[1]

An article in *The Celtic Monthly* tells the legend of the last laird of Borlum in gruesome detail. The writer refers to the laird's brother by both his Gaelic name Alister and the classical name Alexander:

At Raitts, or, as it is now called, Belleville, the last laird of Borlum, Edward Mackintosh, resided. In many respects he excelled most of his forefathers in ferocity, and was one of the most daring robbers that ever lived in the Highlands of Scotland. Within a mile and a half of the mansion house there is an artificial cave in which he and his band found a convenient and secure lurking-place from which to sally forth to rob travellers of their purses, and sometimes of their lives...

In the now thriving village of Kingussie, in the immediate vicinity of the haunt of the Mackintoshes and their associates, there were at the time of which we write, but a few miserable, straggling huts, whose proximity to the cave imposed no check upon Borlum's movements, but rather aided, than obstructed him in his bad and bold career...

A warrant was... issued and placed in the hands of an officer, for the apprehension of Edward Mackintosh and his brother Alexander... Edward contrived to get information of the warrant for his apprehension having been issued... when he summoned a full attendance of his companions in crime to the house at Raitts, where he entertained them to a sumptuous supper and a splendid ball, and early next morning took his departure for the south, escorted a number of miles by his comrades.

He remained in private for some weeks in the house of a friend in Edinburgh, and afterwards made good his escape to France...

...yet his illegitimate brother, Alexander, was apprehended and conveyed to Inverness, and, in due time, tried for robbery and other crimes... Mackintosh produced several witnesses to prove that... he never in his life accompanied Edward in his lawless pursuits – his habits being quiet, peaceful, and honest... ...the jury, after some deliberation, returned a verdict of *Guilty*. The prisoner heard the verdict with the same calm and decent composure which he manifested throughout the trial. The court was crowded to suffocation, and great sympathy was manifested by the majority of the audience for the prisoner, whom they believed to be innocent. The most death-like silence pervaded the Court – every countenance reflected the awful solemnity which all felt, and, in slow and impressive language, the Judge pronounced the

DREADFUL SENTENCE OF THE LAW

the most awful it can inflict – death. ...even in this dreadful hour the prisoner flinched not – no weakness such as might have been expected on such an occasion manifested itself, and his fine handsome form, clad in the humble gray *thickset*, or home-spun corded cloth, stood erect and firm, with the dignity so characteristic of the Highlanders on great and solemn occasions. ... [Mackintosh] solemnly and emphatically denied his guilt... This declaration... produced a strong impression on the audience, which was increased by pity and commiseration for his wife and family. His wife was a mild and gentle creature, and in every respect, a most amiable woman. The prisoner was removed from the bar amidst the prayers and blessings, both loud and deep, of the greater portion of the audience.

At length the day of Mackintosh's execution arrived. How solemn was that dreadful day! Such as could leave their avocations did so in the morning, and paraded the streets in gloomy silence, or, if they spoke, it was only in whispers. By twelve o'clock the streets were almost entirely deserted, and nearly half the population of the town and neighbourhood was collected round the gibbet. It was erected at Muirfield, a little above the town, upon the top of the hill...

At length the culprit, accompanied by two clergymen (the Rev. Messrs. Fraser and Mackenzie), the magistrates, and a strong *posse* of constables, appeared. Mackintosh ascended the fatal ladder with a steady and firm step, and stared vacantly around – he appeared overwhelmed by internal agony – his face was pale, and large drops of perspiration rolled down his cheeks. The Rev. Murdo Mackenzie almost immediately commenced to discharge his sad duty. He began with prayer, to which the prisoner listened with the utmost attention, and his countenance became more settled, as if communing with his Maker and composing his soul. After prayer a psalm was sung, the voices of the assembled multitude rising in solemn consonance into the air...

THE EXECUTIONER

slowly adjusted the noose and pulled down the white cap over his face. ...the culprit's voice broke in accents of piercing agony upon the ear, and sunk into the heart – the last words he uttered were – "Oh, Father, Son, and Holy Ghost, I come." The sound was still murmuring in the breeze when the crowd were startled by a short, sharp knock, or jerk, a something falling, but not distinctly seen... and the culprit's lifeless body was swinging in the wind, and his soul winging its flight into the mansions of eternity. With mingled feelings of sorrow and horror, the multitude slowly and silently dispersed, many, if not most of the company, placing a small piece of bread under a stone, which, according to a superstitious tradition, would prevent after-dreams of the unfortunate Alexander Mackintosh.

After hanging the time required by law, the body was cut down, and according to the sentence, was placed in an iron cage, which was suspended from the top of a post near the gibbet, in order to be a warning and terror, in time coming, to evildoers...

...Highlanders... still secretly, and sometimes openly, maintained their attachment to their chief, and their friendly and brotherly feeling to their namesakes and clansmen...

THE CLAN MACKINTOSH,

in particular, had preserved with the utmost tenacity that spirit of clanship... ...a few of them, resident in and about Inverness, came to the determination of preventing any long continuance of the exposure of the body by cutting it down and interring it. Amongst the number was William Mackintosh, a dyer, better known by the name of "Muckle Willie the Dyster," who from his daring and great strength was looked upon as a leader. The day... had been cold and cloudy, and towards evening showers of drizzling rain began to fall, the wind gradually increased, and about seven o'clock, when the dyer and his companions thought it safe to put their purpose into execution, it swept along in strong gusts. The night was very dark – not a star was to be seen – and as the Mackintoshes stole cautiously out of the town, they, in an undertone congratulated each other that the night was so favourable for their design. They walked circumspectly and slowly until they reached the burn of Aultnaskiach, when they proceeded up the bed of the burn until they arrived at the bridge which crosses it... From that place they crept, rather than walked, over the barren heath, in the direction of the gallows. ... [The Mackintoshes] were almost transfixed with fear, by hearing a short, hard, screeching sound at no great distance from them... For upwards of a minute, the whole party stood fixed and mute – nothing was to be seen – nothing heard, save the whistling of the wind and the grating sound produced by the swinging of

THE IRON CAGE WHEREIN THE BODY

was suspended. The party, however, seeing it like a black cloud hanging in the horizon above their heads, became irresolute and discouraged, and were on the eve of returning home, when Willie broke the silence by a very unceremonious "Pooh, you heard nothing but the wind..." On this they feebly and slowly followed Willie, who sprang to the post, and climbing up with the agility of a cat, was speedily sitting on the top undoing the fastenings, and in a few minutes the cage, with its contents, fell at the feet of his companions with a crash, which they afterwards solemnly declared shook the earth under them. The body was taken out of the cage with the utmost dispatch, and carried across the moor to the bank of the burn. Here they made a hole in the sand with their hands, in which the body was deposited, and covering it over, returned to their dwellings, inwardly congratulating themselves that so disagreeable and dangerous a piece of business was ended... In the morning, when it was discovered that the body of Alister Mackintosh had been taken away during the night, a reward of five pounds was immediately offered to any person who should discover the perpetrators of this daring act... Towards evening, a claimant appeared in the person of Little Tibbie, the wife of Archy the waterman. She had been at Aultnaskiach burn for sand, and to her amazement discovered the stolen body of Mackintosh. She, with great speed repaired to the town to claim the reward, and... roared out as she ran – "Oh, sirs, sirs, Saunders Mackintosh's body!" ...

ANOTHER PARTY OF THE CLAN

headed by the ever ready dyer, proceeded with the greatest expedition to Aultnaskiach burn and removed the body to Campfield, where it was again interred, and allowed to remain...

The widow and children of Alister were amply provided for in every respect by the humane and patriotic Bailie Inglis...

The eldest son, James, entered the Gordon Fencibles... Edward, the second son, entered the navy... There was also a daughter, who, after being educated in all the branches of education suitable for a lady of rank, repaired to the south...

The estate of Raitts subsequently became the property of James Macpherson, Esq., the celebrated translator of the poems of Ossian, who changed its name from Raitts to Belleville – the original name being in his, as well as in the estimation of others, obnoxious. This property he highly cultivated and improved, whereon he built an excellent mansion-house.[2]

"The heir male of the line of Borlum may be found in the descendants of John Mhor Mackintosh and his wife, Mary Fraser, in the State of Georgia," clan historian William Fraser Ross reports. However, Ross points out, "Raigmore is generally looked upon as head of the family of Borlum."[3]

Transitions

When the regiment at Frederica and the garrison at Darien were disbanded, John Mackintosh Mor resumed his career as a gentleman farmer.

As Lachlan McIntosh and his brothers grew into adults, they took an active role in the independence movement in Georgia.

Regiments disbanded

To save money, the British government drastically cut its military forces in Georgia. "About four hundred unemployed veterans, perhaps more than one-quarter of the Georgia labor force, were suddenly and unexpectedly released upon the already distressed economy," reports military historian Larry Ivers. "Georgia's principal industry ceased to exist. Many of the veterans who had originally abandoned their land grants to join the provincial army now applied for charity."[1]

When the Highland Company of Foot was disbanded in 1747 its commander, John Mackintosh Mor, was commissioned as a lieutenant in the 42nd Regiment of Foot and became acting commander of a company garrisoning the fort at Darien.[2]

In addition to his military duties, John Mackintosh Mor continued his lifelong occupation as a gentleman farmer and also operated a store. His son Lachlan, who was a veteran of the regiment at Frederica, probably worked on the family farm and in the store.[3]

Mr. McIntosh's Family
Lachlan McIntosh moves to Charleston: 1748

When Lachlan McIntosh turned 21, he asserted his independence by moving away from his family in the Darien district. McIntosh's biographer Harvey H. Jackson gives the facts:

> ...After the treaty of Aix-la-Chapelle in 1748, British wartime aid to Georgia ended. A recession resulted which caused such an exodus that it seemed the colony "became almost entirely depopulated."
>
> Twenty-one-year-old Lachlan McIntosh took his eleven-year-old brother George and joined other immigrants who went to Charleston.
>
> South Carolina's capital made a lasting impression on the young McIntoshes. The major trading center of the Southern colonies, its businesslike bustle and crowded commercial district showed them just how provincial Georgia was. In addition, the charm and grace of Charleston society set a standard which few American cities were able to match. Its example was not lost on the young men from Darien. George was put in a grammar school and later apprenticed to an architect. Lachlan found employment in a counting house, and though he did not "make his fortune" he at least prospered and was soon able to supply his brother with 100 pounds in Carolina currency as "pocket money" and buy a young Negro to assist him. The brothers were close and the elder always felt protective toward his younger charge, a feeling which characterized their relationship the rest of their lives.
>
> Nearly six feet tall, athletic, described by one friend as the "handsomest man he had ever seen," and possessing a ready wit that in later, more reserved years would be seen only by

close associates, young Lachlan McIntosh began to make friends and slowly wind his way through the labyrinth of Charleston society. His efforts found an influential ally when, during his third year in the city, he met Henry Laurens. A rising member of the merchant elite and a man of considerable political promise, Laurens took a genuine liking to the Georgian, invited him into his home, and, though only three years McIntosh's senior, became a guiding force in his career.

It was a relationship which grew into a long business association, produced a political alliance, and, most importantly, gave Lachlan McIntosh one of the most loyal friendships he was to experience outside his family.

For nearly eight years Charleston was the center of McIntosh's life. He served Laurens well, made the most of the connections he developed, and generally seemed to impress those with whom he dealt...[4]

A nineteenth-century writer offers a more romantic interpretation in *The National Portrait Gallery of Distinguished Americans*:

Lachlin M'Intosh and his brothers were well instructed in English under their mother's care, and after they were received under the patronage of General Oglethorpe, were instructed in mathematics, and other branches necessary for their future military course. But when General Oglethorpe left Georgia, all hope, and perhaps all wish, for remaining longer attached to his regiment, ceased in the young men.

William became an active and successful agriculturist, and Lachlin, in search of a wider field of enterprise, went to

Charleston in South Carolina, where his father's gallantry, and his father's misfortunes, drew upon him the attentions of many; and his fine and manly appearance, his calm, firm temper, his acquirements for his opportunity, procured for him first the acquaintance, and then the warm friendship, of Henry Laurens, the most distinguished and most respectable merchant at that time in Charleston, afterwards president of congress, and first minister from the United States to Holland. Mr. Laurens took the young M'Intosh into his counting-house and into his family, and with him he remained some years. In association with this enlightened and respectable gentleman, Mr. M'Intosh had an opportunity of studying men and books, and of filling up the blanks in his education.

From some repugnance to commerce, arising probably from his early military propensities, he did not adopt the pursuit of his friend and patron, but after spending some years in Charleston, he returned to his friends still residing on the Altamaha...[5]

South Carolina historian George C. Rogers points out: "As a merchant, Henry Laurens trained many boys as clerks in his counting house. His wharf on Cooper River with its auxiliary buildings was an early business school."[6]

While Lachlan and George McIntosh were in Charleston, their brother Phineas died in Darien in about 1749 at about age 17.

The end of an era: 1749

In April of 1749 the Frederica regiment was disbanded and the company that had been garrisoning the fort at Darien was disbanded; as a result John Mackintosh Mor was no longer needed as a lieutenant in the company. Military historian Larry Ivers analyzes the historical significance of the occasion:

> The year 1733 began a military era on the southern frontier, and the year 1749 brought that era to a close. The War of Jenkins's Ear-King George's War was over, Georgia's career as a military buffer colony was ended, and the drums of the British regulars and Georgia provincials were silent.
>
> Naïve visions of fortified frontier villages populated with free yeomen farmers, carrying a hoe in one hand and a musket in the other, evaporated forever in July 1749 when the Georgia trustees legalized the use of Negro slave labor.
>
> No longer were settlements strategically located for defense; of all of the towns settled during the military era, only Savannah, Augusta, and Darien survived. The military no longer served as Georgia's principal industry. Regimental and provincial officers no longer exercised excessive influence in civil affairs. Military command of the southern frontier was transferred from the commander of the forces in Georgia to the governor of South Carolina, and Georgia became a military backwater; only a few regulars and a single crew of boatmen were maintained on duty.
>
> The sixteen years between 1733 and 1749 were also James Edward Oglethorpe's personal era. During most of that period he was the dominant personality, both politically and militarily, on the southern frontier. By utilizing varying degrees of diplomacy and armed force, he worked to carry out Britain's imperialistic policy, much of which he had formulated...

In 1749, at the age of fifty-three, Oglethorpe abandoned the social and professional seclusion that he had entered in 1746 as a result of public criticism concerning his actions during the Jacobite Rebellion, and he began devoting his energies to Parliamentary work. Over one-third of his life still lay ahead of him, and he would enjoy additional successes and suffer new failures. However, he severed all contact with Georgia, attending his last trustees' board meeting on 16 March 1749.[7]

Ann McIntosh marries Robert Baillie: 1751

At Darien, John Mackintosh Mor's daughter Ann married Robert Baillie, a Highlander who had immigrated to Darien under John Mor's leadership and who had commanded Fort Barrington on the Altamaha River. After the Independent Company of Foot was disbanded and Fort Barrington was abandoned, Robert and Ann Baillie grew rice on her land at the headwaters of the Sapelo River.[8]

John Mackintosh goes to Jamaica

John Mackintosh Mor's third son, John, moved from Georgia to Jamaica in around 1752. Although he never returned from Jamaica, he continued to correspond with his family.[9]

Highlanders want Gaelic-speaking minister

Gaelic remained the language of the Highlanders at Darien for many years. Sixteen years after Darien was founded, a memorial of the inhabitants of Darien requested a Gaelic-speaking Christian minister from Scotland because many of them did not speak English.

John McLeod, the Presbyterian minister who accompanied the first emigrants to Georgia, had moved to South Carolina after five years in Darien. After he left, Darien residents depended on the Rev. Thomas Bosomworth, an assistant chaplain to the regiment at Frederica, to officiate at occasional religious services. A chapel that had been built in Darien when the Highlanders first arrived was replaced by a meeting house eight miles north of Darien before 1750. When Bosomworth returned to England in 1752, the inhabitants of Darien were left utterly destitute of any minister of the gospel. The nearest minister was in Savannah.

"I assure you the people here will miss your absence very much, having no other clergyman to apply to," wrote John Mackintosh Mor to Bosomworth. "A good many souls here lay under for want of one to teach them the way of salvation ... I assure you, there is not a place in America wants it more."[10]

Plantations flourish

Many Highlanders received land grants in the District of Darien as rewards for their service in the Battle of Bloody Marsh and other action against Spanish forces on the southern frontier of America.

John Mackintosh Mor was granted property along the Sapelo River known as the "Borlum lands" because he was related to the Mackintoshes of Borlum in the Highlands of Scotland. His sons William, Lachlan and George and his daughter Ann also received land grants, and one of William's plantations was named Borlum.

When large-scale slaveholding was allowed in Georgia in the 1750s, Highlanders who had opposed slavery in 1739 became slave owners. Taking advantage of slave labor, landowners in coastal Georgia became prosperous planters.

Mr. and Mrs. Lachlan McIntosh go to Georgia

While living in South Carolina, Lachlan McIntosh met Sarah Threadcraft of Williamsburg. He married her on New Year's Day of 1756, and they relocated to the Darien District later that year.

When Lachlan's younger brother George finished his apprenticeship to an architect in Charleston, Lachlan "brought him back to Georgia and got him appointed commissary of supplies for Troops in garrison at Frederica, and other ports dependent thereon." Lachlan also "instructed him in geometry and surveying and furnished him with books for those purposes, in order that George might by those means acquire a more perfect knowledge of his own Country and have an opportunity of getting the most valuable lands at that early period for himself" under Lachlan's advice and direction.[11]

When George showed inclination to be a planter, as Lachlan recalled later in a legal deposition, Lachlan was "his security in Charleston for the first parcel of Negroes said George ever purchased, with which and his own industry he acquired all the property he ever possessed. Of all these advantages he made the best use and became one of the most thriving planters in this State, uniformly ascribing all his successes to [Lachlan's] steady friendships to him, and always declaring and looking upon [Lachlan] in the light of a father and a tryed friend, rather than a brother."[12]

Biographer Harvey Jackson reports a blessed event in 1757:

Shortly after the new year began, Sarah McIntosh gave birth to her first child, a healthy son. The boy was named John after his grandfather, an ancient name for a new and promising generation. Now a man with new family responsibilities, Lachlan McIntosh's activities took on an added sense of purpose.[13]

Lachlan and Sarah's second son—named Lachlan and called Lachlan Jr. or Lackie—was born about a year later. Over the years, their marriage would produce eight children.

In 1758 Lachlan McIntosh acquired a thousand acres on an island across the north branch of the Altamaha River from Darien; the tidal flow of the waterways of the island made the property suitable for growing rice. Starting with sixteen slaves, he developed the land into a plantation.[14] Later that year, he and his older brother William McIntosh acquired a thousand acres on Broughton and Doboy Islands.

Eventually acquiring fourteen thousand acres of land and sixty slaves, Lachlan McIntosh experienced success as a rice planter.

McIntosh and Laurens form partnerships

In 1763 Henry Laurens – Lachlan's mentor in Charleston – acquired nine hundred acres on Broughton Island adjacent to the McIntosh property. As an absentee landowner, Laurens depended on Lachlan to help manage the Broughton Island property.

Laurens and Lachlan made other joint investments in various enterprises in coastal Georgia.

Lachlan sent his oldest son John to school in Charleston under Laurens' supervision.[15]

Tales about Rory McIntosh

Roderick "Rory" McIntosh, the son of John Mackintosh Mor's first cousin Benjamin, became a legendary character. Rory's plantation Mallow adjoined Fairhope, home of John Mackintosh Mor's son William McIntosh.

ON ONE OCCASION, Rory and William went together to Charleston. Along the way, they stayed several days at a house near Jacksonborough. Rory fell in love with a young woman who lived there, and assigned William to seek permission from the girl's father for Rory to marry her. The father thanked William for the honor, but reported that the girl was already engaged to a local man.

When Rory got the bad news, he declared, "I will beat him and spit on her intended."

William asked, "But why? He has not injured you."

Rory answered, "He is my rival, and I will disgrace him."

William argued with Rory for a long time before convincing him to continue on their journey.

DURING A SLAVE INSURRECTION near Savannah, Rory led a party who attacked the slave's fortification. One of his men fired his musket and stepped behind a tree to reload.

Rory asked him, "And can't you, like a brave man, load your musket in the road?"

Rory was wounded during the skirmish, and for the rest of his life one of his shoulders was disfigured. The attackers succeeded in taking the slaves prisoner.

ANOTHER ADVENTURE ENSUED when Rory went to apprehend a Creek Indian who had committed murder. Armed with a Scottish dirk, Rory intimidated a group of the murderer's friends, seized the murderer, and brought him to justice. In an alternate version of the tale, Rory killed the murderer on the spot.

ALTHOUGH NOT WEALTHY, Rory made a comfortable living by raising cattle at Mallow. Once, when Florida was still possessed by Spain, he conducted a cattle drive to St. Augustine. He was paid in dollar coins, which he put in a canvas bag on his horse. On his ride home over rough paths, he had almost reached Mallow when the canvas tore and some of the dollars fell onto the ground. He secured the dollars left in the bag but did not look for the coins that had fallen.

When he needed money several years later, he went to the spot where the bag had broken, and picked up as much money as he needed. Later, when he needed money again, he used the same resource.

WHEN RORY LEARNED that a new acquaintance was fond of shooting birds, Rory said, "My young friend, I see you are a sportsman and I love you for it."

Rory hunted game not only for "amusement," according to his friend John Couper, but also for "business," which "supplied a bountiful table."

Rory often told tales of shooting on Blackbeard Island near Darien, where the huge flocks of ducks and geese made so much noise on a frosty morning that the hunters could hardly hear each other talk.

RORY LOVED DOGS and owned hounds and setters, including a dog named Luath. (The Scots Gaelic word "luath" is an adjective meaning "quick, fast"). One time, Rory made a considerable bet that Luath could follow his trail three miles and retrieve a gold doubloon that Rory had hidden under a log. Luath set off on Rory's trail but returned without the doubloon.

Rory rushed to the hiding spot and found that Luath had scratched under the log. Rory turned over the log, but the doubloon was no longer there.

Then Rory noticed a man in the distance splitting rails. Rory approached the man, drew his dirk, and swore he would kill him unless the man returned the doubloon. The man gave Rory the doubloon, and explained that he had seen Rory put something under the log and had gone to investigate and had found the gold.

Rory then tossed the doubloon back to the man. "Take it, vile caitiff," said Rory. "It was not the pelf, but the honor of my dog I cared for."

HIS SCOTS HIGHLANDER heritage was important to Rory. He carried a dirk, went about attended by bagpipers, and spoke Gaelic. When he met a Scots immigrant who was ignorant of Gaelic, Rory told the immigrant, "I pity you, but you may be an honest man for all that."

Being a grandson of the illustrious Jacobite Brigadier William Mackintosh of Borlum, Rory kept alive romantic notions of the royal Stuarts and Bonnie Prince Charlie, surreptitiously referred to as "The Young Gentleman."[16]

John McIntosh moves to Indian country

Rory McIntosh's brother John McIntosh married Margaret McGillivray, whose family was involved in trading with the southern Indians. John and Margaret and their teenage son William went to live in Indian country in the 1760s. John established a trading post called McIntosh Bluff on the Tombigbee River.[17]

John Mackintosh Mor dies: 1761

In his later years John Mackintosh Mor concentrated on his farming operations. He had returned to a lifelong occupation: he had been "a gentleman farmer" in Scotland and his uncle Brigadier William Mackintosh had published a treatise on agriculture. Local historian Bessie Lewis gives the location of John Mackintosh Mor's farm and assesses the family patriarch's social status:

> John McIntosh Mohr, returned at last from Spanish prison, settled on Black Island, near where the highlanders landed when they came to Barnwell's Bluff... He was appointed Conservator of the Peace for Darien, and continued to be leader and mentor of his people.[18]

Another Georgia historian, Alexander Lawrence, gives this interpretation of John Mackintosh Mor's final years:

> Eventually Captain Mackintosh returned to Georgia after long confinement in the "common Jayl" at San Sebastian where his fare, he complained, was "no more than bread and water." Broken in health, the Highland chief lived out his remaining years at Darien, passing most of his time, tradition tells us, be-

neath a great oak along the salt creek that flowed by his home.[19]

John Mackintosh Mor died in 1761 at his farm Essick on the Sapelo River. A contemporary observer wrote that the 63-year-old patriarch died "prematurely… by the quackery and ignorance of the first Doctor who ever tried to make his fortune amongst the honest patriarchs."[20]

He was buried in the old city cemetery in Darien along with his wife Marjory, who died "after May 1741."[21]

McIntosh family takes part in politics

In 1764, two members of Lachlan McIntosh's extended family were elected as delegates from St. Andrews Parish to the Commons House of Georgia. One of them was his younger brother George McIntosh. His brother-in-law Robert Baillie, husband of his only sister Ann, was the other delegate.

Lachlan himself served as tax collector and justice of the peace. He also supervised an effort to rebuild Fort Frederica, where he had been stationed as a cadet at the time of the Battle of Bloody Marsh. He used his surveying skills on road projects and to lay out a new plan of the town of Darien based on Oglethorpe's original concept.

Creek chief tries to shoot Rory McIntosh

Roderick McIntosh narrowly escaped death in 1768. He antagonized an Indian while he was on an assignment with Edward Barnard and George Galphin to mark the boundary between Indian territory and lands open to settlement.

Georgia historian Edward J. Cashin, who says Roderick was "known as Old Rory for his ferocious temper," tells what happened:

> ...Three Creek chiefs – the Young Lieutenant, Salechee, and Blue Salt – led the wary Creek contingent.
>
> The Indians argued that Upton Creek at the proposed town of Wrightsborough should be the boundary set by the 1763 treaty. "Old Rory" contended with increasing vehemence that the south fork some twenty-five miles upstream should be the source of the line.
>
> One of the chiefs took a decided aversion to McIntosh, pointed his gun at the Scotsman, and pulled the trigger.
>
> Fortunately for the cause of peace along the frontier and to the enormous relief of Galphin, Barnard, and presumably McIntosh, the gun misfired.
>
> Galphin calmed the hot heads, and they settled on Williams Creek by way of compromise.[22]

Political intrigue engulfs Georgia

When George McIntosh and his brother-in-law Robert Baillie attempted to take their seats in the Commons House in 1768, their election was challenged. Before the controversy was resolved, the royal governor of Georgia dissolved the Assembly because the Georgians had supported their fellow colonists in Massachusetts against British policies.

In 1770, Lachlan McIntosh was elected as a delegate to the Commons House. Once again, the Georgians flexed their political muscle and the royal governor dissolved the Assembly.

Later, George McIntosh was elected as a delegate from St. Mary's parish, where he had recently purchased property.

George McIntosh marries into influential family

In 1772, John Mackintosh Mor's son George McIntosh married Ann Priscilla Houston, whose family was among the social elite in colonial Georgia. Shortly afterwards, George McIntosh and his brother-in-law Sir Patrick Houston were elected to the Commons House as delegates from St. Andrew's parish. At least one of them continued to serve until the American Revolution brought an end to British government in Georgia. In 1774, George McIntosh was among the citizens who met in Savannah to protest British policies.

Lachlan McIntosh befriends William Bartram

Lachlan McIntosh offered his hospitality to naturalist William Bartram in the spring of 1773, and they continued to correspond throughout their lifetimes. Georgia historian Edward J. Cashin tells the tale:

> Traveling alone on horseback, he [William Bartram] followed the high road south from Midway. After ten miles the plantations became fewer and the road worse... With the poor road and the gathering dusk, William managed to lose his way completely and blundered along through swamps and creeks, characteristically unafraid and trusting to Providence. Sure enough, he saw a light glimmering through the darkness and followed it to a house, where he stayed the night...
>
> ... [The man] whose "glimmering light" rescued Bartram had his overseer guide the botanist through a dangerous

swamp and point him in the direction of Darien. He rode through a forest of pines, crossed a branch of the Sapelo River and arrived at a small plantation on the South Newport River, the home of Donald McIntosh, one of the original emigrants from Inverness. Bartram described how the "venerable grey headed Caledonian" came out to welcome him to his home and hospitality. He admired the primitive simplicity of the household. A furious storm broke out while they were at a meal of venison; a bolt of lightning set a tree ablaze less than forty yards away... Although William may have never visited Donald McIntosh again, he never forgot him. Writing to Lachlan McIntosh in 1796, he said, "Give respects to Good Old Don'd McIntosh at the Swamp between Sapello and the great swamp where I had shelter during the tremendous thunder storm."[23]

After delivering a message from Governor Wright to Robert Baillie – the husband of John Mackintosh Mor's daughter Ann – at the headwaters of the Sapelo River, Bartram proceeded to Lachlan McIntosh's home on the banks of the Altamaha River at Darien.[24] William Bartram and Lachlan McIntosh had an acquaintance in common: Henry Laurens of Charleston, who was something of a father figure to both of them.

Cashin continues the tale:

Of the many people he met and friends he made, with the exception of Mary Lamboll Thomas, William Bartram liked Lachlan McIntosh best. They hit it off from the first. Many years later Bartram's heart filled with sentiment when he recollected that meeting: "When I came up to the door, the friendly man, smiling, and with a grace and dignity peculiar to himself, took me by the hand and accosted me thus, 'Friend Bartram, come under my roof and I desire you to make my house your home as long as convenient to yourself; remember, from this moment that you are part of my family, and on my part I shall endeavor to make it agreeable.'" There were already ten in the McIntosh household so the invitation to Bartram represented a triumph of hospitality over housekeeping. The eight children paraded by to be introduced to their guest: John, at sixteen the oldest, then in chronological order, Lachlan, William, George, Henry, John Hampton, Hester and Catherine. William [Bartram] got along famously with them, and the warmth of their regard drew him to Darien for prolonged visits during his explorations. William later recalled "those happy scenes, happy hours which I enjoyed with your family." He especially liked the conversations he had with McIntosh in the evenings, the "improving Philosophic conversation," as he phrased it. The discussions touched on William's favorite theme, the working out of the designs of Providence. He exclaimed, "O my Friend, what a degree of intellectual enjoyment our nature is susceptible of when we behold and contemplate the Moral system impressed on the Human Mind by the Divine Intelligence" ...

William encountered so many McIntoshes that he had difficulty sorting them out. The Scots compounded the problem by insisting on using the names of fathers and grandfathers. For example, Lachlan and Sarah named their sons John, Lachlan, William, George, Henry and John Hampton. Lachlan's older brother William, and his wife, Jane Mackay, also named their sons John, William, Lachlan, and George... [William McIntosh's children] Lachlan and Hester both married Baillies. Margery had recently married James Spalding... and the couple lived on nearby St. Simon's Island... Barbara, the youngest daughter, compounded the confusion by marrying yet another William McIntosh. Even Bartram, who knew them well, could get confused. Years later, when a young man approached Bartram at his home in Kingsessing, William recognized him as a McIntosh but could not place him. "Lachlan," the young man answered. That narrowed the possibilities but remained imprecise. "Lachlan's or William's?" "William's," came the answer. William Bartram paid him a nice compliment: "His countenance and manners bespeaks the Gentleman."

Sixteen-year-old Jack [Lachlan and Sarah's oldest son John] expressed keen interest in Bartram's expedition. The idea of exploring a vast and mysterious wilderness appealed to his sense of adventure. Would William permit Jack to accompany him on his trip to the interior of Georgia? William expressed his entire satisfaction at the idea... Proud father Lachlan was all for it; Sarah McIntosh needed further gentle persuasion.[25]

Jack McIntosh travels with William Bartram

After pondering Jack's request while Bartram was off exploring along the Altamaha for about a week, Sarah McIntosh gave Jack permission to accompany Bartram on his travels. Jack and Bartram set out from Darien on May 1, 1773. As they rode across Georgia, Bartram jotted notes on the farms they passed and the herds of deer and flocks of turkeys they saw. In a few days, beautiful springtime weather turned terribly hot and dry. They came across Governor Wright on his way to a congress in Augusta and learned that several fine horses belonging to the group escorting the governor "died in the Road by reason of the Heat and drouth." They stayed a few days at Indian trader George Galphin's post at Silver Bluff on the South Carolina side of the Savannah River. On May 14 they crossed the river to Augusta and joined a large expedition sent to survey lands recently ceded to Georgia by the Creek and Cherokee nations. Edward Barnard led the group of at least eighty men, including contingents of Creek and Cherokee warriors, along the main Creek trading path out of Augusta. Two days of traveling brought them to Wrightsborough in the Georgia piedmont. As they followed the old Cherokee trail westward out of Wrightsborough to a camp on Williams Creek in June, Bartram noted outcroppings of rock.[26] Cashin describes the botanist's activities:

> After caring for his horse and pitching his tent, Bartram liked to roam about in hopes of discovering new plants, a joy shared by few others as he admitted. At times the agreeable young McIntosh would go along. They found the yellow root plant at the Williams Creek camp. The next morning after Young Warrior's daily ritual, they saddled up and resumed their deliberate pace along the south side of the Little River. They crossed numerous small streams, thought by Bartram to be branches of the Ogeechee but most likely tributaries of the Little River...
>
> The next day they crossed the north fork of the Little River and entered a region described by the surveyors as heavily timbered in oak, hickory, walnut, chestnut and tulip poplar, interspersed with pine and canebrakes. The dark topsoil of six to seven inches covered a bed of red clay. Bartram expressed

awe at the most magnificent forest he had ever seen. He measured several oaks that had a circumference of thirty feet...

They passed a buffalo lick... on the way to their destination, the Great Buffalo Lick. Bartram called the latter "an extraordinary place" [covering] an acre and a half with some depressions five and six feet deep. Buffalo had roamed this region as recently as Oglethorpe's time. By 1773 they were gone... Deer and other animals kept the ground clear [because] sodium sulphate in the soil appealed to animals...

The significance of the Great Buffalo Lick, as Bartram's contemporaries knew, was that it lay in a gap of the ridge that divided the waters of the Savannah River from those of the Oconee-Altamaha basin. Bartram referred to it as the Great Ridge, probably because of its cartographical importance rather than its topographical elevation. In truth, there is little to distinguish this ridge from the innumerable long hills of the piedmont. However, the treaty writers regarded the ridge as a crucial dividing place... [As the surveyors tried to mark the boundary of the land ceded by the Creeks] the question led to a lively dispute between Young Warrior and Philip Yonge that must have reminded Barnard of Rory McIntosh's near-fatal dispute [in 1768]. Bartram witnessed the surveyor pointing in one direction and the chief in another... The angry Creeks said this was a trick to cheat them out of their lands... Barnard... respected the Native Americans' intimate knowledge of the region. He decided to follow the direction of Young Warrior rather than that of his professional. Bartram approved the decision and praised "the complaisance and prudent conduct of the Colonel."[27]

When the expedition divided into two teams, Bartram and Jack McIntosh accompanied Barnard's team as it explored the northern line of the ceded lands. When they reached a marked tree that showed where Creek hunting grounds ended and Cherokee hunting grounds began, the contingent of Creek warriors left the expedition. Barnard and the contingent of Cherokee warriors continued to follow the boundary of the ceded lands to the junction of the Tugaloo and Keowee rivers. The beautiful landscape impressed Bartram: "A pleasant morning attended by the feather'd inhabitants of these shady retreats, with joyful song invites us forth, the elevated face of this Hilly country breathes an elastic pure air, inspiring health and activity." **Cashin, *William Bartram*, 64.** After traveling for two days, the team made camp on a tributary of the Broad River while the Cherokee warriors hunted deer and turkey. Cashin reports that Bartram went looking for new plants and when he returned to camp:

> ...he found Jack McIntosh, his "philosophic companion," raptly engaged in the study of little hills of gravel here and there in the shoals of the swift, flowing stream. He thought the hills were made by crawfish as tiny citadels against the numerous predatory goldfish. The swift-darting, beautifully colored goldfish so fascinated Bartram that he drew a picture of one... The little hills in the water are made by minnows hatching their eggs.[28]

Bartram and Jack McIntosh rode with Colonel Barnard over rolling hills to the Tugaloo River and to the Indian town of Tugaloo in the foothills of the Cherokee mountains. In July, they reached the junction of the Tugaloo and the Savannah rivers, where Bartram commented on the flourishing rhododendron, mountain laurel and hydrangeas. Two young Indians harpooned dozens of trout and bream; one trout was two feet long and weighed about fifteen pounds, Bartram said. The Indian and white members of the expedition shared a meal of barbecued fish to celebrate the success of their mission. The next morning the Indians went their way and the white men headed back toward Augusta. Barnard and Bartram continued to Savannah. News soon reached them that two young Indians from their expedition had been murdered by settlers on the Broad River, disrupting the colonial governor's plans for developing the ceded lands.[29]

Georgians support Continental Congress

When the first Continental Congress met in Philadelphia in 1774, Georgia did not participate. By 1775, friction between the American colonies and the English government had reached a crisis. Although Boston was the center of attention, Georgia played a supportive role. McIntosh County historian Buddy Sullivan describes the situation:

> On January 1, 1775, several months before Lexington and Concord, the Darien Committee gathered at the Meeting House on the Broad Road north of Darien and appointed Lachlan McIntosh as their leader and spokesman. The group expressed full support for their defiant colonial brethren in New England. The Darien Committee met again on January 12 to reaffirm its support of the revolutionary cause as well as choose local del-

egates to the Provincial Congress which was to be convened in Savannah.[30]

Darien Committee opposes slavery

The Darien Committee's most remarkable declaration was a call to free the slaves in Georgia, an eerie echo of the petition against slavery signed by the Scots at Darien in 1739. John Mackintosh Mor had led the generation who opposed slavery in 1739, and his son Lachlan McIntosh led the generation who opposed slavery in 1775.

Even though Lachlan McIntosh owned about sixty slaves and his brother George owned about forty slaves, Lachlan recognized that slavery was untenable. The Darien Committee called slavery "an unnatural practice... founded in injustice and cruelty, and highly dangerous to our liberty (as well as our lives) debasing part of our fellow creatures below men, and corrupting the virtue and morals of the rest, and is laying the basis of that liberty we contend for... upon a very wrong foundation."[31]

Biographer Harvey Jackson gives context to McIntosh's decision to take part in the independence movement:

> Because of his well-known reluctance to intervene in colonial politics, McIntosh's role as leader of the Darien committee comes as something of a shock... Still, it would have been difficult for him to have done otherwise. The McIntoshes had come to Georgia, as refugees from English-dominated Scotland, to serve the Trustees, not the crown. After royalization, that allegiance was transferred to the colony, Georgia; and

there is nothing to indicate that, in the process, they developed a similar attachment to George III.[32]

Savannah historian Alexander Lawrence quoted Lachlan McIntosh's own words revealing his attitude toward independence from Britain. Apparently referring to his Mackintosh forebears' role in the Jacobite risings, Lachlan McIntosh told a fellow Georgian: "Neither we or our fathers could Bear, or even understand aright, that Medley of all Governments the British, with its numberless Offices and Pomp."[33]

Directory

Brief biographical sketches can be used in place of an index. The reader can learn which events a particular person was involved in, and then read the relevant chapters.

MACKINTOSH, AENEAS, 22nd Chief of Clan Mackintosh, sometimes called by the Gaelic name Angus. He was related to the McIntosh men in Georgia through the 16th Chief of Clan Mackintosh.

He served in the British army in colonial America, was commissioned lieutenant at the Palachacola ranger fort on the Savannah River in 1732, and was one of twenty-five men who accompanied Oglethorpe on a visit to the Creek nation in 1739.

In 1740, he returned to Scotland, and succeeded as the Chief of Clan Mackintosh when his older brother died. He married Anne Farquharson in 1741.

In the Rising of 1745, he served in the government army while his wife raised the Mackintoshes for the rebels. He surrendered to rebel forces at Dornoch in March of 1746. He was set free when the Rising ended with the Battle of Culloden in April of 1746, and managed to save the Mackintosh estate at Moy from destruction.

He died in 1770 and was succeeded by his nephew, also named Aeneas.

MACKINTOSH, AENEAS (1751-1820), 23rd Chief of Clan Mackintosh. He succeeded as Chief when his uncle died in 1770. When the American Revolution began, he raised a company for the 71st Regiment of Foot and was given the rank of captain. He fought in many of the most significant battles of the war. He was taken prisoner when Cornwallis surrendered at Yorktown in October of 1781.

He returned to Scotland in 1783 and managed the farming and forestry operations on his estates. An accidental fire destroyed the Mackintosh manor house, and he constructed the fourth building known as Moy Hall in 1800.

King George created Aeneas a baronet in 1812 and he became known as Sir Aeneas.

MACKINTOSH, ANNE (1725–1784), known as Colonel Anne, married Aeneas the 22nd Chief of Clan Mackintosh on January 14, 1741. She was the daughter of John Farquharson of Invercauld, the chief of that branch of Clan Chattan. John Farquharson had fought under the command of Brigadier William Mackintosh of Borlum in the Rising of 1715 and had been taken prisoner with the other Clan Chattan soldiers at Preston.

In the early stages of the Rising of 1745, Aeneas raised a company of militia for the government. His wife Anne, at the age of 20, raised the clan for the Jacobites without any hindrance from him.

Lady Anne Mackintosh hosted Prince Charles and a few attendants at Moy, home of the Chief of Clan Mackintosh, on February 16, 1746. A government attempt to capture the Prince was thwarted in the Rout of Moy. When Aeneas surrendered to Jacobite forces, according to the official clan historian, Prince Charles sent Aeneas Mackintosh to Moy to be held prisoner by his wife Lady Anne Mackintosh.

On April 17, one detachment of government troops was sent to Moy to bring in all the cattle while another detachment was sent to take Lady Anne Mackintosh to Inverness.

She remained in custody at Inverness for six weeks.

In 1748, Lady Anne Mackintosh visited London and attended a ball given by William Augustus, the Duke of Cumberland.

When her husband Aeneas died in 1770 and was succeeded by his nephew Aeneas, Lady Anne Mackintosh moved to Edinburgh. She died on March 2, 1784.

MACKINTOSH, ANGUS. SEE **MACKINTOSH, AENEAS**, 22nd Chief of Clan Mackintosh.

MACKINTOSH, BENJAMIN, the natural son of Brigadier William Mackintosh of Borlum. He was one of the founders of Darien led by his cousin John Mackintosh Mor in 1736. He was the father of Roderick "Rory" McIntosh, John McIntosh, Winnewood McIntosh, and others. He was the grandfather of William McIntosh, a British emissary to the Creek Indians, and the great-grandfather of Chief William McIntosh. He moved from Darien to Charleston in October of 1740.

MACKINTOSH, JOHN (1698 or 1700-1761), known as John Mackintosh Mor, teenage soldier in the Jacobite Rising of 1715, leader of the colonists at Darien in 1736, father of Colonel William McIntosh, General Lachlan McIntosh, and others.

He was taken prisoner in the invasion of Florida in 1740 and held in a Spanish jail. He was released in 1743 and returned to his family in Georgia.

He died in 1761 at his farm near Darien and was buried in the old city cemetery in Darien.

MACKINTOSH, MARJORY FRASER (1701-?), wife of John Mackintosh Mor. She was born in 1701 at Boleskine, a daughter of John Fraser of Garthmore and Elizabeth Fraser of Errogy. She married John Mackintosh on March 4, 1725. **Gladstone, Family Group Record.**

After her husband was taken prisoner in the Battle of Mosa in 1740, Marjory took three of their children to Palachacola and sought refuge from John Mackintosh, a ranger captain who was distantly related to her husband.

Based on the scant source material available, biographer Harvey H. Jackson concludes that Marjory reunited with her husband after he was released from prison in Spain. After reporting that Marjory "returned to Darien to await her husband's release" (4), Jackson reports: "Sometime between 1744 and 1748 John McIntosh was released and the family reunited... During the next four years Lachlan McIntosh remained with his family at Darien..." (5).

Family genealogist Mattie Gladstone records Marjory's date of death as "after May, 1741," the place of death as Darien and the location of the grave as the old city cemetery in Darien.

MACKINTOSH, WILLIAM (c. 1663-1743), Jacobite officer in the Risings of 1715 and 1719. William Mackintosh was the great-grandson of the founder of the Mackintosh of Borlum family. He was often referred to as Borlum, although in 1715 he was technically the younger of Borlum because his father was still alive. The lands of Borlum were on the River Ness about five miles to the southwest of Inverness. William Mackintosh possessed the estate of Raits in Badenoch.

William Mackintosh was born around 1663. He received a Master of Arts at Kings College and was considered a man of polite education and good knowledge. In 1686 he became the father of a natural son, Benjamin.

He received military training in France and in the Guards of King William and Queen Anne. While in England, he married Mary Reade of Ipsden, Oxfordshire. Before their marriage in 1688, she had been a Maid of Honour to Princess Anne, later Queen Anne.

The couple had five children: Lauchlan, 5th of Borlum; Shaw, 6th of Borlum; Winwood; Maria Forbes; and Helen.

William Mackintosh became a Jacobite agent and was sent on a mission to James Edward Stuart's residence at Bar-le-Due in Lorraine. By the time William Mackintosh returned to Scotland in 1714, he was an experienced soldier in the French service.

Brigadier William Mackintosh of Borlum remained in Scotland after the Battle of Glenshiel in 1719. He was imprisoned in 1729 for his part in the Rising of 1715. He refused to take an oath of allegiance to the king, and spent his last fifteen years as a prisoner in Edinburgh Castle. He died January 7, 1743, at the age of about 80 (Mackintosh; MacKintosh, "Brigadier;" Moncreiffe; Rose; Sullivan).

McINTOSH, GEORGE (1739-1779), youngest son of John Mackintosh Mor.

He accompanied his brother Lachlan to Charleston in 1748 and they lived there together until 1756.

George married Ann Priscilla Houston, a member of one of Georgia's most prominent families. George became a successful planter and established Rice Hope at the head of the Sapelo River.

George's wife died in 1777, so when George died in 1779 at the age of 40 his estate passed to his 7-year-old son John Houston McIntosh.

McINTOSH, JOHN, known as John McIntosh Mohr, SEE **MACKINTOSH, JOHN,** known as John Mackintosh Mor.

McINTOSH, LACHLAN (1727-1806), Continental General. He was born in Scotland, on March 5, 1727, in Achugcha, near Raits in Badenoch, the second son of Marjory and John Mackintosh Mor.

When Lachlan was 8 years old, his father led a group of Highlanders who sailed to America and founded the town of Darien, Georgia.

In February of 1740, 13-year-old Lachlan and his sister Anne went to the orphanage at Bethesda, near Savannah. Lachlan joined the regiment at St. Simons as a cadet shortly before the Battle of Bloody Marsh at St. Simons in 1742.

When Lachlan McIntosh turned 21, he asserted his independence by moving away from his family in the Darien district. Bringing his younger brother George with him, he moved to Charleston and stayed there nearly eight years.

While living in South Carolina, Lachlan McIntosh met Sarah Threadcraft of Williamsburg. He married her on New Year's Day of 1756, and they relocated to the Darien District later that year. Lachlan experienced success as a rice planter and made joint investments with Henry Laurens in various enterprises in coastal Georgia.

Lachlan and Sarah's first child was born early in 1757 and was named John after his grandfather John Mackintosh Mor.

Their second son – named Lachlan and called Lachlan Jr. or Lackie – was born about a year later. In 1759 their third son was born and was given the esteemed family name William. Over the years, their marriage would produce five more children: daughters Hester and Catherine and younger sons George, Henry Laurens and John Hampden, called Hampden.

In 1770, Lachlan McIntosh was elected as a delegate to the Commons House.

Lachlan McIntosh offered his hospitality to roving naturalist William Bartram in the spring of 1773, and they continued to correspond throughout their lifetimes.

In January of 1775, Lachlan served as leader of the Darien Committee, which issued a declaration against slavery.

Georgians opposed to British rule called a Second Provincial Congress in the summer of 1775. Lachlan McIntosh remained the leader of the Darien Committee that elected delegates to the Provincial Congress. The committee selected Lachlan, his older brother William, and his younger brother George as delegates. On July 4, 1775, the Provincial Congress declared its support for the Continental Congress and established itself as Georgia's revolutionary government.

Congress elected Lachlan McIntosh to lead the first Continental battalion in Georgia in January of 1776. Lachlan was promoted to Brigadier General on September 16, 1776.

Lachlan died at his house in Savannah on February 20, 1806. He was buried at the old Christ Church cemetery, now named Colonial Park.

McINTOSH, RODERICK (died 1782), known as "Rory." He was in his late teens or early twenties when he emigrated from Scotland in 1736 with his father Benjamin, brother John and sister Winnewood. Their family was among the group of Highlanders – led by Benjamin's cousin John Mackintosh Mor – who founded Darien on the Georgia coast.

Rory fought at the Battle of Mosa in Florida in 1740. Conditions deteriorated in Darien following the debacle at Mosa, and Rory's father was among the discontented Highlanders who left Darien in the 1740s. Rory's brother John became an Indian trader on the southern frontier. Roderick and his sister Winnewood remained on the family's plantation, Mallow, near Darien. Rory became a legendary character.

Remaining loyal to Great Britain during the American Revolution, Rory found refuge in the British territory of East Florida in 1777. After the war ended badly for his side, Rory decided to return to Scotland. He survived the voyage across the Atlantic but before he reached his boyhood home he died aboard ship at Gravesend, England, in 1782.

McINTOSH, WILLIAM (1726-1801), eldest son of John Mackintosh Mor, brother of General Lachlan McIntosh and father of Colonel John McIntosh. He fought in the Battle of Mosa in 1740 and the Battle of Bloody Marsh in 1742.

He married Mary Jane Mackay. William became a successful planter at Fair Hope on the Sapelo River and participated with his brothers in political activities.

As the commander of a troop of light horse in the opening period of the American Revolution, he conducted campaigns on the southern frontier.

His daughter Margery married James Spalding and lived on St. Simons Island; her son Thomas Spalding recorded the history and legend of his family in early Georgia.

Notes

The Jacobite Risings of 1715 and 1719

[1] Edward J. Cashin, *Lachlan McGillivray, Indian Trader* (Athens: University of Georgia Press, 1992), 13.
[2] Margaret Mackintosh of Mackintosh, *The History of Clan Mackintosh and Clan Chattan* (Edinburgh: The Pentland Press Limited, 1997), 44; Bessie Lewis, *They Called Their Town Darien (*Darien, Ga.: The Darien News, 1975), 16; Buddy Sullivan, *Early Days on the Georgia Tidewater* (Darien: McIntosh County Board of Commissioners, 1990), 33.
[3] Alexander Mackintosh Shaw, *Historical Memoirs of the House and Clan of Mackintosh and of the Clan Chattan*, 1880 (Markham, Va.: Apple Manor Press, 2017), 422.
[4] Theo Aronson, *Kings Over the Water* (London: Cassell, 1979), 91.
[5] Margaret Mackintosh, *History of Clan Mackintosh*, 44-45.
[6] Margaret Mackintosh, *History of Clan Mackintosh*, 45.
[7] Angus MacKintosh, "Brigadier MacKintosh of Borlum," *The Celtic Monthly* (Jan. 1903), 73.
[8] D. Murray Rose, *Historical Notes or Essays on the '15 and '45* (Edinburgh: William Brown, 1896), 80-82.
[9] Margaret Mackintosh, *History of Clan Mackintosh*, 45-46.
[10] Angus MacKintosh, "Brigadier MacKintosh of Borlum," *The Celtic Monthly* (Jan. 1903), 74.
[11] Angus MacKintosh, "Brigadier MacKintosh of Borlum," *The Celtic Monthly* (Jan. 1903), 74.
[12] William Seymour, *Battles in Britain 1066-1746* (London: Sidgwick & Jackson, 1989), 2: 187-90.
[13] Margaret Mackintosh, *History of Clan Mackintosh*, 46.
[14] Seymour, *Battles in Britain*, 2: 187-91.

[15] Margaret Mackintosh, *History of Clan Mackintosh*, 46-49.

[16] David Dobson, *Directory of Scots in the Carolinas, 1680-1830* (Baltimore: Genealogical Publishing, 1986), 162-64.

[17] William Fraser Ross, "Family of Mackintosh of Borlum," *Clan Chattan* 1: 6 (1939), 186-87.

[18] Margaret Mackintosh, *History of Clan Mackintosh*, 28-29.

[19] Ross, "Family of Mackintosh of Borlum," 186.

[20] Iain Moncreiffe and David Hicks, *The Highland Clans* (New York: Bramhall House, 1977), 128; Sullivan, *Early Days on the Georgia Tidewater*, 36.

[21] Ross, "Family of Mackintosh of Borlum," 185; Albert S. Britt Jr., and Lilla M. Hawes, eds., "The Mackenzie Papers, Part II," *Georgia Historical Quarterly* 57, no. 1 (1973), 110-11.

[22] Lewis, *Darien* 16; David Dobson, *Scottish Emigration to Colonial America, 1607-1785* (Athens: University of Georgia Press, 1994), 118.

[23] Angus MacKintosh, "Brigadier MacKintosh of Borlum," 75.

[24] J.J. Galbraith, "The Battle of Glenshiel, 1719," (Presented to the Gaelic Society of Inverness, Nov. 23, 1928, Rpt. Bruceton Mills, W. Va.: Unicorn Limited, c. 1994), 296-97.

[25] Frank McLynn, *The Jacobites* (London: Routledge & Kegan Paul, 1985), 104.

[26] Seymour, *Battles in Britain*, 2: 198-200.

[27] Galbraith, "The Battle of Glenshiel," 304.

[28] Galbraith, "The Battle of Glenshiel," 306.

[29] Galbraith, "The Battle of Glenshiel," 307-10.

[30] Margaret Mackintosh, *History of Clan Mackintosh*, 49.

[31] Angus MacKintosh, "Brigadier MacKintosh of Borlum," 75.

[32] Ross, "Family of Mackintosh of Borlum," 186.

[33] Ross, "Family of Mackintosh of Borlum," 187.

[34] Ross, "Family of Mackintosh of Borlum," 187.

[35] Margaret Mackintosh, *History of Clan Mackintosh*, 52.

[36] Britt and Hawes, "The Mackenzie Papers, Part II," 111.

[37] Alexander A. Lawrence, "General Lachlan McIntosh and His Suspension from Continental Command During the Revolution," *Georgia His-*

torical *Quarterly* 38.2 (1954), 105; Britt and Hawes, "The Mackenzie Papers, Part II," 111.

[38] Mattie Gladstone, Family Group Record for John Mor McIntosh, not published; Britt and Hawes, "The Mackenzie Papers, Part II," 111.

The settlement of Georgia

[1] Larry Ivers, *British Drums on the Southern Frontier* (Chapel Hill: The University of North Carolina Press, 1974), 9.

[2] Ivers, *British Drums*, 23, 27.

[3] Ivers, *British Drums*, 10.

[4] Ivers, *British Drums*, 11-16.

[5] Ivers, *British Drums*, 27-28.

[6] Ivers, *British Drums*, 31-37.

[7] Ivers, *British Drums*, 37-39.

[8] Dobson, *Scottish Emigration* 118.

[9] Lewis, *Darien*, 11.

[10] Edward J. Cashin, *Lachlan McGillivray, Indian Trader* (Athens: University of Georgia Press, 1992), 12-14.

[11] Margaret Mackintosh, *History of Clan Mackintosh*, 52-53.

[12] Moncreiffe and Hicks, *The Highland Clans*, 128; Sullivan, *Early Days on the Georgia Tidewater*, 36.

[13] Gladstone, Family Group Record.

[14] Lewis, *Darien*, 1-2, 11-12.

[15] Sullivan. *Early Days on the Georgia Tidewater*, 19.

[16] Edward J. Cashin, *Lachlan McGillivray, Indian Trader* (Athens: University of Georgia Press, 1992), 16.

[17] Cashin, *Lachlan McGillivray*, 16-17.

[18] Cashin, *Lachlan McGillivray*, 17-18.

[19] Thomas Spalding, "Lachlan McIntosh, 1725-1806: Soldier" in *The National Portrait Gallery of Distinguished Americans* (New York: Arno Press and The New York Times, 1970), 3: 110.

[20] Lawrence S. Rowland, Alexander Moore and George C. Rogers Jr., *The History of Beaufort County, Volume I, 1514-1861* (Columbia: University of South Carolina Press, 1996), 141; Ivers, *British Drums,* 17.
[21] Ivers, *British Drums,* 12.
[22] William Fraser Ross, "Family of Mackintosh of Borlum," *Clan Chattan* 1, no. 6 (1939), 187.
[23] Britt and Hawes, "The Mackenzie Papers, Part II," 111.
[24] Anthony W. Parker, *Scottish Highlanders in Colonial Georgia* (Athens: University of Georgia Press, 2002), 66-67.
[25] *Colonial Records of Georgia,* 21: 443-46.
[26] *Colonial Records of Georgia* 4: 165.
[27] Lewis, *Darien,* 16-17.
[28] *Colonial Records of Georgia,* 3: 427-28.

The struggle for the southern frontier

[1] Larry E. Ivers, *British Drums on the Southern Frontier (*Chapel Hill: The University of North Carolina Press, 1974)*,* 86-88.
[2] "Ranger's Report of Travels with General Oglethorpe in Georgia and Florida, 1739-1742" in *Travels in the American Colonies*, ed. Newton D. Mereness (New York: Antiquarian Press, 1961), 218-21.
[3] "Oglethorpe's Treaty with the Lower Creek Indians," *Georgia Historical Quarterly* 4.1 (March 1920), 8.
[4] Larry E. Ivers, *Colonial Forts of South Carolina 1670-1775* (Columbia: University of South Carolina Press, 1970), 70; *Colonial Records of the State of Georgia* (New York: AMS Press, 1970), 4: 511, 522.
[5] Larry E. Ivers, *British Drums on the Southern Frontier (*Chapel Hill: The University of North Carolina Press, 1974), xi, 90-91.
[6] George White, *Historical Collections of Georgia* (Baltimore: Genealogical Publishing Company, 1969), 334-35; Thomas Spalding, "Lachlan McIntosh" in *The National Portrait Gallery of Distinguished Americans* (New York: Arno Press and The New York Times, 1970), 3: 103.
[7] Mills Lane, ed., *General Oglethorpe's Georgia: Colonial Letters. 1733-1743* (Savannah: The Beehive Press, 1975), 2: 437-39.

[8] Ivers, *British Drums,* 101.
[9] Bessie Lewis, *They Called Their Town Darien* (Darien, Ga.: The Darien News, 1975), 18-19.
[10] Thomas Spalding, "Sketch of the life of General James Oglethorpe presented to the Georgia Historical Society" in *Collections of the Georgia Historical Society* v. 1. (Savannah: Georgia Historical Society, 1840), 271.
[11] Ivers, *British Drums,* 106-07.
[12] Ivers, *British Drums,* 107-08.
[13] Ivers, *British Drums,* 114-16, 119-22.
[14] White, *Historical Collections of Georgia,* 470.
[15] Lewis, *Darien,* 19.
[16] *Colonial Records of Georgia* 35: 336-37.
[17] Ivers, *British Drums,* 122.
[18] Spalding, "Oglethorpe," 271.
[19] Ivers, *British Drums,* 122-23.
[20] Lane, *General Oglethorpe's Georgia,* 2: 536.
[21] Lewis, Darien, 19.
[22] White, *Historical Collections of Georgia,* 334-35.
[23] Qtd. in Sullivan, *Early Days on the Georgia Tidewater,* 34.
[24] Anthony W. Parker, *Scottish Highlanders in Colonial Georgia* (Athens: University of Georgia Press, 2002), 82-83; Jackson, *Lachlan McIntosh,* 4.
[25] Ivers, *British Drums,* 133.
[26] Parker, *Scottish Highlanders,* 83; Cashin, *Lachlan McGillivray,* 36.
[27] *Colonial Records of Georgia* 35: 335-37.
[28] *Colonial Records of Georgia* 35: 340-43.
[29] *Colonial Records of Georgia* 35: 345-46.
[30] Parker, *Scottish Highlanders,* 85-86.
[31] White, *Historical Collections of Georgia,* 334; Jackson, *Lachlan McIntosh,* 4-5.
[32] Ivers, *British Drums,* 152-59.
[33] Ivers, *British Drums,* 159-61.
[34] Ivers, *British Drums,* 161.

[35] Ivers, *British Drums,* 163-65.
[36] "Ranger's Report," 235.
[37] Ivers, *British Drums*, 165; Spalding, "Oglethorpe," 284.
[38] Ivers, *British Drums*, 165-67.
[39] Ivers, *British Drums*, 172.
[40] "Ranger's Report," 234-35.
[41] Spalding, "Oglethorpe," 283-84.
[42] Lewis, *Darien* 22-23.
[43] Alexander R. MacDonell, "The Settlement of the Scotch," *Georgia Historical Quarterly* 20.3 (1936): 251, 256-58.
[44] Ivers, *British Drums,* 165-67.
[45] "Ranger's Report," 235.
[46] Ivers, *British Drums,* 168-72.
[47] Spalding, "Lachlan McIntosh," 103.
[48] Parker, *Scottish Highlanders in Colonial Georgia,* 82-83; Jackson, *Lachlan McIntosh,* 4-5; Ivers, *British Drums,* 186, 193-94; White, *Historical Records of Georgia,* 335.

The Jacobite Rising of 1745

[1] Margaret Mackintosh of Mackintosh, *The History of Clan Mackintosh and Clan Chattan* (Edinburgh: The Pentland Press Limited, 1997), 52.
[2] Edward J. Cashin, *Lachlan McGillivray, Indian Trader* (Athens: University of Georgia Press, 1992), 35.
[3] Margaret Mackintosh, *History of Clan Mackintosh,* 54.
[4] Angus MacKintosh, "Lady MacKintosh of the '45,'" *The Celtic Monthly* (Dec.1902), 45; Robert McGillivray, "Colonel Anne of the '45," *Clan Chattan: The Journal of Clan Chattan* 11, no. 2 (2002), 72-73.
[5] McGillivray, "Colonel Anne," 72.
[6] Margaret Mackintosh, *History of Clan Mackintosh,* 54.
[7] James Johnstone, *Memoirs of the Rebellion in 1745 and 1746 by the Chevalier de Johnstone,* Rpt. in *Culloden 1746: The Last Highland Charge* (Stratford-upon-Avon: Cromwell Productions, 1993), 11.
[8] Margaret Mackintosh, *History of Clan Mackintosh,* 55.

[9] Norman H. MacDonald, *The Clan Ranald of Knoydart & Glengarry* (Edinburgh: Norman H. MacDonald, 1979), 88.
[10] William Seymour, *Battles in Britain 1066-1746* (London: Sidgwick & Jackson, 1989), 2: 206.
[11] Michael Barthorp, *The Jacobite Rebellions, 1689-1745* (London: Osprey, 1982), 12; Seymour, *Battles in Britain,* 208; Johnstone, *Memoirs of the Rebellion,* 16.
[12] Cashin, *Lachlan McGillivray,* 53.
[13] Barthorp, *Jacobite Rebellions,* 28.
[14] Cashin, *Lachlan McGillivray,* 53.
[15] Ivers, *British Drums,* 200-01.
[16] Cashin, *Lachlan McGillivray,* 53-54.
[17] Johnstone, *Memoirs of the Rebellion,* 43-46.
[18] Barthorp, *Jacobite Rebellions,* 13.
[19] Barthorp, *Jacobite Rebellions,* 13.
[20] Frank McLynn, *The Jacobites* (London: Routledge & Kegan Paul, 1985), 65-66.
[21] McLynn, *The Jacobites,* 155.
[22] Bruce Lenman, *The Jacobite Clans of the Great Glen, 1650-1784* (Aberdeen: Scottish Cultural Press, 1995) 126-27.
[23] Margaret Mackintosh, *History of Clan Mackintosh,* 55.
[24] Qtd. in MacKintosh, "Lady MacKintosh," 45.
[25] McGillivray, "Colonel Anne," 73-74.
[26] David Smurthwaite, *The Ordnance Survey Complete Guide to the Battlefields of Britain* (London: Webb & Bower, 1987), 205.
[27] Barthorp, *Jacobite Rebellions,* 14.
[28] McGillivray, "Colonel Anne," 74.
[29] Margaret Mackintosh, *History of the Clan Mackintosh,* 55, 57.
[30] McGillivray, "Colonel Anne," 75-76.
[31] Angus MacKintosh, "Lady MacKintosh," 46-47.
[32] Fitzroy Maclean, *Highlanders: A History of the Scottish Clans* (New York: Penguin, 1995), 213.
[33] Johnstone, *Memoirs of the Rebellion,* 66.

[34] Margaret Mackintosh, *History of Clan Mackintosh*, 57; Norman H. MacDonald, *The Clan Ranald of Knoydart & Glengarry* (Edinburgh: Norman H. MacDonald, 1979), 96.
[35] Johnstone, *Memoirs of the Rebellion*, 73-74.
[36] Barthorp, *Jacobite Rebellions*, 14; MacDonald, *Clan Ranald*, 96.
[37] Qtd. in MacDonald, *Clan Ranald*, 96.
[38] Bruce Lenman, *The Jacobite Clans of the Great Glen* (Aberdeen: Scottish Cultural Press, 1995), 127.
[39] Johnstone, *Memoirs of the Rebellion*, 74.
[40] McGillivray, "Colonel Anne," 76.
[41] Angus MacKintosh, "Lady MacKintosh," 47.
[42] Peter Harrington, *Culloden 1746: The Highland Clans' Last Charge* (London: Osprey, 1991), 44.
[43] Harrington, *Culloden*, 52-60.
[44] Harrington, *Culloden*, 60-68.
[45] Harrington, *Culloden*, 78-83; McGillivray, "Colonel Anne," 76.
[46] Margaret Mackintosh, *History of Clan Mackintosh*, 59-61.
[47] Angus MacKintosh, "Lady MacKintosh," 47.
[48] Peter Young and John Adair, *From Hastings to Culloden* (Kineton: The Roundwood Press, 1979), 267.
[49] Margaret Mackintosh, *History of Clan Mackintosh*, 62-63.
[50] Angus MacKintosh, "Lady MacKintosh," 47-48.
[51] McGillivray, "Colonel Anne," 77.
[52] Margaret Mackintosh, *History of Clan Mackintosh*, 63-64.
[53] McGillivray, "Colonel Anne," 77.
[54] Theo Aronson, *Kings Over the Water* (London: Cassell, 1979), 158.
[55] Angus MacKintosh, "Lady MacKintosh," 48.
[56] Angus MacKintosh, "Lady MacKintosh," 48.

The Last Laird of Borlum

[1] William Fraser Ross, "Family of Mackintosh of Borlum," *Clan Chattan* 1, no. 6 (1939), 188.

² "Traditions of the Mackintoshes of Borlum," *The Celtic Monthly* 13, no. 9 (June 1905), 165-68, and 13, no. 10 (July 1905), 187-89.
³ Ross, "Family of Mackintosh of Borlum," 188.

Transitions

¹ Larry E. Ivers, *British Drums on the Southern Frontier* (Chapel Hill: The University of North Carolina Press, 1974), 203.
² Larry E. Ivers, *British Drums on the Southern Frontier* (Chapel Hill: The University of North Carolina Press, 1974), 206.
³ Harvey Hardaway Jackson III, *Lachlan McIntosh and the Politics of Revolutionary Georgia* (Athens: University of Georgia Press, 2003), 5.
⁴ Jackson, *Lachlan McIntosh,* 5-6.
⁵ Thomas Spalding, "Lachlan McIntosh, 1725-1806: Soldier," in *The National Portrait Gallery of Distinguished Americans* (New York: Arno Press and The New York Times, 1970), 3: 103-04.
⁶ George C. Rogers Jr., "A Tribute to Henry Laurens," *South Carolina Historical Magazine* 92 no. 4 (1991), 269-70.
⁷ Ivers, *British Drums,* 214-15.
⁸ Edward J. Cashin, *William Bartram and the American Revolution* (Columbia: University of South Carolina Press, 2000), 33.
⁹ Buddy Sullivan, *Early Days on the Georgia Tidewater: The story of McIntosh County & Sapelo,* (Darien: McIntosh County Board of Commissioners, 1990), 34-35.
¹⁰ *Colonial Records of Georgia* 27: 258-60.
¹¹ "Case of George McIntosh," *Georgia Historical Quarterly* 3, no. 3 (Sept. 1919), 136.
¹² "Case of George McIntosh," 136.
¹³ Jackson, *Lachlan McIntosh,* 8.
¹⁴ Sullivan, *Early Days on the Georgia Tidewater,* Appendices, 1.
¹⁵ Cashin, *Bartram,* 34, 37; Sullivan, *Early Days on the Georgia Tidewater*, Appendices, 1.
¹⁶ George White, *Historical Collections of Georgia* (Baltimore: Genealogical Publishing Company, 1969), 470-74.

[17] "Captain William McIntosh;" Sullivan, *Early Days on the Georgia Tidewater,* 34-37.

[18] Bessie Lewis, *They Called Their Town Darien* (Darien, Ga.: The Darien News, 1975), 24.

[19] Alexander A. Lawrence, "General Lachlan McIntosh and His Suspension from Continental Command During the Revolution," *Georgia Historical Quarterly* 38.2 (1954), 104-05.

[20] Sullivan, *Early Days on the Georgia Tidewater*, 46.

[21] Mattie Gladstone, Family Group Record, on file at the Lower Altamaha Historical Society in Darien, Ga.

[22] Edward J. Cashin, *William Bartram and the American Revolution* (Columbia: University of South Carolina Press, 2000), 33, 60.

[23] Cashin, *William Bartram,* 31-35.

[24] Cashin, *William Bartram,* 35; Sullivan, *Early Days on the Georgia Tidewater,* 56.

[25] Cashin, *William Bartram,* 35-37.

[26] Cashin, *William Bartram,* 41-60.

[27] Cashin, *William Bartram,* 61-63.

[28] Cashin, *William Bartram,* 65.

[29] Cashin, *William Bartram,* 66-67.

[30] Sullivan, *Early Days on the Georgia Tidewater*, 57.

[31] Sullivan, *Early Days on the Georgia Tidewater,* 57.

[32] Jackson, *Lachlan McIntosh,* 25.

[33] Lawrence, "General Lachlan McIntosh," 107.

Bibliography

Aronson, Theo. *Kings Over the Water: The Saga of the Stuart Pretenders.* London: Cassell, 1979.

Barthorp, Michael. *The Jacobite Rebellions, 1689-1745.* London: Osprey, 1982.

Britt Jr., Albert S., and Lilla M. Hawes, eds. "The Mackenzie Papers, Part II." *Georgia Historical Quarterly* 57, no. 1 (1973): 113-115.

"Case of George McIntosh," *Georgia Historical Quarterly* 3, no. 3 (Sept. 1919), 136.

Cashin, Edward J. *Lachlan McGillivray, Indian Trader: The shaping of the Southern Colonial Frontier.* Athens: University of Georgia Press, 1992.

--- *William Bartram and the American Revolution.* Columbia: University of South Carolina Press, 2000.

"Colonel John McIntosh laid to rest for the third time in McIntosh Co." *The Darien News* 28 Oct. 2010: 1+

Colonial Records of the State of Georgia (CRG), 28 vols. 1904-10. New York: AMS Press, 1970.

Dobson, David. *Directory of Scots in the Carolinas, 1680-1830.* Baltimore: Genealogical Publishing, 1986.

---. *Scottish Emigration to Colonial America, 1607-1785.* Athens: University of Georgia Press, 1994.

Galbraith, Dr J.J. "The Battle of Glenshiel, 1719." Presented to the Gaelic Society of Inverness, Nov. 23, 1928. Rpt. Bruceton Mills, W. Va.: Unicorn Limited, c. 1994.

Gladstone, Mattie. Notes, manuscripts and photocopies related to McIntosh genealogy. The Ridge, Darien, Georgia: unpublished, personal communication, 1980 - 2002.

---. Family Group Record for John Mor McIntosh. Copies may be available at the Lower Altamaha Historical Society office at Fort King George Historic Site at Darien, Georgia.

---. Genealogical chart showing descendants of William Mackintosh, 3rd Proprietor of Borlum. Copies may be available at the McIntosh County Historical Society office at Fort King George Historic Site at Darien, Georgia.

Harrington, Peter. *Culloden 1746: The Highland Clans' Last Charge*. London: Osprey, 1991.

Hawes, Lilla M., ed. *Collections of the Georgia Historical Society Vol. XII: The Papers of Lachlan McIntosh, 1774-1779*. Savannah: Georgia Historical Society, 1957.

---, ed. *University of Georgia Libraries Miscellanea Publications, No. 7: Lachlan McIntosh Papers in the University of Georgia Libraries*. Athens: University of Georgia Press, 1968.

Ivers, Larry E. *British drums on the Southern Frontier: The military colonization of Georgia, 1733-1749*. Chapel Hill: The University of North Carolina Press, 1974.

---. *Colonial Forts of South Carolina 1670-1775*. Columbia: University of South Carolina Press, 1970.

Jackson III, Harvey Hardaway. *General Lachlan McIntosh, 1727-1806: A Biography*. Diss. University of Georgia, 1973. Athens: University of Georgia, 1973.

---. *Lachlan McIntosh and the Politics of Revolutionary Georgia*. 1979. Athens: University of Georgia Press, 2003.

"John McIntosh." *GlynnGen.com Coastal Georgia Genealogy & History*. 10 March 2011 <http://www.glynngen.com/military/amrev/glynn/mcintoshjno.htm>

Johnstone, James. *Memoirs of the Rebellion in 1745 and 1746 by the Chevalier de Johnstone*. 1820. Rpt. in *Culloden 1746: The Last Highland Charge*. Stratford-upon-Avon: Cromwell Productions, 1993.

Lane, Mills, ed. *General Oglethorpe's Georgia: Colonial Letters. 1733-1743*. 2 vols. Savannah: The Beehive Press, 1975.

Lawrence, Alexander A. "General Lachlan McIntosh and His Suspension from Continental Command During the Revolution." *Georgia Historical Quarterly* 38.2 (1954): 101-141.

Lenman, Bruce. *The Jacobite Clans of the Great Glen, 1650-1784*. 1984. Aberdeen: Scottish Cultural Press, 1995.

Lewis, Bessie. *They Called Their Town Darien*. Darien, Ga.: The Darien News, 1975.

"Lt. Benjamin McIntosh." *The Briskey Crossroads.*10 March 2011 <http://briskeycrossroads.com/McI ntosh.html>

MacDonald, Norman H. *The Clan Ranald of Knoydart & Glengarry: A history of the MacDonalds or MacDonells of Glengarry*. Edinburgh: Norman H. MacDonald, 1979.

MacDonell, Alexander R. "The Settlement of the Scotch." *Georgia Historical Quarterly* 20.3 (1936): 250-62.

MacKintosh, Angus. "Brigadier MacKintosh of Borlum." *The Celtic Monthly* Jan. 1903: 73-75.

---. "How the feud between the Camerons and Mackintoshes was ended." *The Celtic Monthly* Apr. 1903: 122-24.

---. "Lady MacKintosh of the '45.'" *The Celtic Monthly* Dec.1902: 45-49.

Mackintosh of Mackintosh, Margaret, revised by Lachlan Mackintosh of Mackintosh, 30th Chief of Mackintosh. *The History of*

Clan Mackintosh and Clan Chattan. Edinburgh: The Pentland Press Limited, 1997.

Maclean, Fitzroy. *Highlanders: A History of the Scottish Clans*. New York: Penguin, 1995.

McGillivray, Robert. "A Tribute to Virtue." *Clan Chattan: The Journal of Clan Chattan* XII.5 (2011): 269-271.

---. "Colonel Anne of the '45." *Clan Chattan: The Journal of Clan Chattan* XI.2 (2002): 70-79.

McLynn, Frank. *The Jacobites*. London: Routledge & Kegan Paul, 1985.

Moncreiffe of that Ilk, Sir Iain and David Hicks. *The Highland Clans: The dynastic origins, chiefs and background of the Clans and of some other families connected with Highland history*. 1967. New York: Bramhall House, 1977.

"Oglethorpe's Treaty with the Lower Creek Indians." *Georgia Historical Quarterly* 4.1 (March 1920): 3-16.

Parker, Anthony W. *Scottish Highlanders in Colonial Georgia: The recruitment, emigration, and settlement at Darien, 1735-1748*. Athens: University of Georgia Press, 2002.

"Ranger's Report of Travels with General Oglethorpe in Georgia and Florida, 1739-1742." *Travels in the American Colonies*. 1916. Ed. Newton D. Mereness. New York: Antiquarian Press, 1961: 215-36.

Rogers Jr., George C. "A Tribute to Henry Laurens." *South Carolina Historical Magazine* 92 no. 4 (1991): 269-276.

Rose, D. Murray. *Historical Notes or Essays on the '15 and '45*. Edinburgh: William Brown, 1896.

Ross, William Fraser. "Family of Mackintosh of Borlum." *Clan Chattan* I.6 (1939): 180-90.

Rowland, Lawrence S., Alexander Moore and George C. Rogers Jr. *The History of Beaufort County, Volume I, 1514-1861*. Columbia: University of South Carolina Press, 1996.

Seymour, William. *Battles in Britain 1066-1746*, v. 2. London: Sidgwick & Jackson, 1989.

Shaw, Alexander Mackintosh. *Historical Memoirs of the House and Clan of Mackintosh and of the Clan Chattan*, 1880. Markham, Va.: Apple Manor Press, 2017.

Smurthwaite, David. *The Ordnance Survey Complete Guide to the Battlefields of Britain*. London: Webb & Bower, 1987.

Spalding, Thomas. "Lachlan McIntosh, 1725-1806: Soldier." *The National Portrait Gallery of Distinguished Americans*, v. 3. 1867. New York: Arno Press and The New York Times, 1970: 99-110.

---. "Sketch of the life of General James Oglethorpe presented to the Georgia Historical Society." *Collections of the Georgia Historical Society* v. 1. Savannah: Georgia Historical Society, 1840: 240-95.

Sullivan, Buddy. *Early Days on the Georgia Tidewater: The story of McIntosh County & Sapelo*. Darien: McIntosh County Board of Commissioners, 1990.

---. Supplemental Appendices. *Early Days on the Georgia Tidewater: The story of McIntosh County & Sapelo*. 1991.

"Traditions of the Mackintoshes of Borlum." *The Celtic Monthly* 13, no. 9 (June 1905): 165-68, 187-89 and 13, no. 10 (July 1905)): 187-89.

White, George. *Historical Collections of Georgia*. 1855. Baltimore: Genealogical Publishing Company, 1969.

Young, Peter and John Adair. *From Hastings to Culloden (Battlefields in Britain)*. Kineton: The Roundwood Press, 1979.

What? No Index?

A Directory starting on page 187 contains brief biographical sketches that can be used in place of an index. The reader can learn which events a particular person was involved in, and then read the relevant chapters.

www.ingramcontent.com/pod-product-compliance
Lightning Source LLC
Chambersburg PA
CBHW072000290426
44109CB00018B/2082